"I'm a huge fan of the Herbivorous Butcher's fool-your-friends vegan meats. Like so many others, I've been moving to a more plant-based diet, and now I've got more tools (and fewer excuses!) for kicking an unhealthy meat habit. Aubry and Kale have done the nearly impossible: They've created a cookbook that breaks the mold."

—Rocco DiSpirito, chef, cookbook author, and television personality

"The Herbivorous Butcher is a pioneer in the plant-based deli space. Their vegan deli meats and cheeses have given me and my clients a fix for all our favorite meals. Their passion for sustainability and love for our world translates through their products. I love this book!"

—Charity Morgan, author of *Unbelievably Vegan*

"Kale, Aubry, and their team are doing such amazing work, and I love their creativity! I personally eat a primarily plant-based diet and always love stopping by their storefront in Minneapolis. I'm excited to try these recipes at home. I truly love the passion in these recipes and know they will be an inspiration to many for more delicious plant-based foods and healthier lifestyles!"

—Sean Sherman, CEO and founder, Owamni, The Sioux Chef, and Indigenous Food Lab

THE
HERBIVOROUS
BUTCHER
COOKBOOK

THE
HERBIVOROUS
BUTCHER

COOKBOOK

75+ Recipes for Plant-Based Meats
and All the Dishes You Can Make with Them

by Aubry and Kale Walch

with Sandra Soria and Danny Seo

Photographs by Rikki Snyder

CHRONICLE BOOKS
SAN FRANCISCO

Library of Congress Cataloging-in-Publication Data is available.

ISBN 978-1-7972-1195-4

Manufactured in China.

Prop styling by **Rikki Snyder.**

Food styling by **Leslie Orlandini.**

Design by **Vanessa Dina.**

Typesetting by **Frank Brayton.**

The photographer wishes to thank Chronicle Books for the wonderful opportunity to work on this book, Aubry and Kale Walch for entrusting their vision with me throughout the process, Leslie Orlandini and Kersti Bowser for their hard work and amazing talents in helping make the photos come to life, Rebecca French for her immense support throughout the shoot and for opening up her studio doors so we could make this project happen, and Danny Seo for connecting all of the dots and paving the way for this entire opportunity. Thank you all so very much.

Benihana is a registered trademark of Noodle Time, Inc.; Beyond Meat is a registered trademark of Beyond Meat, Inc.; BOCA is a registered trademark of Kraft Foods, Inc.; *Diners, Drive-Ins and Dives* is a registered trademark of Television Food Network, G.P.; Follow Your Heart VeganEgg is a registered trademark of Old Friends Holdings, LLC; Food Network is a registered trademark of Television Food Network, G.P.; Grey Poupon is a registered trademark of Kraft Foods Group Brands LLC; Impossible is a registered trademark of Impossible Foods Inc.; Instant Pot is a registered trademark of Instant Brands Inc.; JUST Egg is a registered trademark of Eat Just, Inc.; Kickstarter is a registered trademark of Kickstarter, PBC; Kimlan is a registered trademark of Kimlan Foods Co.; Lightlife is a registered trademark of Greenleaf Foods, SPC; McDonald's is a registered trademark of McDonald's Corporation; MorningStar Farms is a registered trademark of Kellogg North America Company; Ritz Crackers is a registered trademark of Mondelēz International; Sizzler is a registered trademark of Sizzler USA Franchise, Inc.; Spam is a registered trademark of Hormel Foods, LLC; *The Price Is Right* is a registered trademark of FremantleMedia Netherlands B.V.; Tofurky is a registered trademark of Turtle Island Foods, SPC; *X-Files* is a registered trademark of Twentieth Century Fox Film Corporation.

10 9 8 7 6 5 4 3 2 1

Chronicle books and gifts are available at special quantity discounts to corporations, professional associations, literacy programs, and other organizations. For details and discount information, please contact our premiums department at corporatesales@chroniclebooks.com or at 1-800-759-0190.

Chronicle Books LLC
680 Second Street
San Francisco, California 94107

www.chroniclebooks.com

To people, animals, and the planet

Listen, we don't want to get all harsh right off the bat, but . . .

This is next-level important, so listen up (pretty please): The need for meat alternatives has never been greater. Global demand for meat has tripled in the last forty years, causing dramatic and unsustainable increases in greenhouse gas emissions, deforestation, and water pollution. Industrial animal production intensifies pressures on land, water, fertilizer, feed, and fuel. We know, big bummer.

Now the good news: A modest reduction in the consumption of animal products would not only spare billions of animals from inhumane treatment every year, but eating less meat and dairy would also have a huge environmental impact at a time when the world urgently needs to reduce greenhouse gas emissions to avert catastrophic climate change. The Herbivorous Butchers are responding to this call to action because together we can all change the world—one meal at a time!

And the best news of all: All of our plants-only meat recipes serve up optimum amounts of protein and B vitamins that many meat alternatives lack, as well as modest levels of monounsaturated fats that help reduce cholesterol and satisfy your hunger. Translated: You will feel really good, body and soul. We dedicate this book to positive environmental change and to you, our readers.

About the Herbivorous Butcher

Located in Minneapolis—which is pretty deep in meat-and-potatoes country— the Herbivorous Butcher was founded in 2014 by the brother-sister team of Kale and Aubry Walch. It holds the honor of being the first vegan butcher shop in the world. Today, vegetarians, vegans, and omnivores alike crowd around the Herbivorous Butcher's big white deli cases to check out what's new, ask for meal recommendations, or pick up their favorite order. It's a destination for all things vegan but also a friendly, kosher, neighborhood spot where people meet up and curious customers ask a lot of crazy questions (which are always welcome).

From meaty provisions such as porterhouse steak, Korean barbecue ribs, pastrami, jalapeño Cheddar brats, and chorizo, to creamy vegan cheeses including Camembert, garlic pepper Havarti, Muenster, and feta, the Herbivorous Butcher continually shocks and delights patrons with how realistic these meat and cheese alternatives are. Even Guy Fieri raved at how delicious the meat-free meats were on his hit Food Network TV show *Diners, Drive-Ins and Dives*.

The Herbivorous Butcher quickly went national, shipping their creations to all fifty states and Puerto Rico, and has been expanding its new take-and-bake offerings, hot meals, subs, and hot sandwiches to keep up with the growing demand for more ready-to-eat choices. Ever since they started at the Minneapolis Farmers Market in 2014, Aubry and Kale have tirelessly concocted new recipes with flavor profiles that are now so complex that they put fine wines to shame.

You might wonder, why would anyone make plant-based meats when brands like Impossible, Beyond Meat, MorningStar Farms, Lightlife, and so many others exist? The answer is simple: The handcrafted Herbivorous Butcher products are tastier, fresher, and cleaner. And because they're made in small batches, it's easier for Aubry and Kale to have fun experimenting, stay ahead of the curve, and ship out new products all the time!

The Butchers start with all-natural ingredients (things you can buy from your local co-op) and carefully craft them into whatever product customers might dream up. It's always done in small, taste-tested batches. This means you get food that's healthier, lower in fat, and cholesterol-free. It's food that contains complete, meat-free protein that leaves you feeling fine and full of energy.

Rather than reconstituting products with high-tech microwaves, Aubry and Kale found just the right combination of steaming, searing, boiling, and baking to perfect those elusive meat and cheese flavors *and* textures. From the mouthwatering, melty goodness of mozzarella to the decadent succulence of filet mignon, the quality, love, and bold innovations of every Herbivorous Butcher product is unmistakable—and, might we add, irresistible.

ABOUT THE HERBIVOROUS BUTCHER

And now, Aubry and Kale would like to share some of their favorite recipes with you for the first time ever. Have fun trying them out, eating them, serving them. And, please, stop by and let the Butchers know how you like the results. Enjoy!

Meet Aubry

Guam native. Big sister. Animal saver. Activist. Vegan.

My brother and I are transplants from the tropical Pacific island of Guam to the mostly arctic lake country of Minnesota. I was born on Guam and lived there until my family moved to the Midwest when I was thirteen years old and Kale was a six-month-old baby.

On Guam, three things are important—family, food, and food with family. Guam's food culture is very meat-heavy. I grew up eating meat with nearly every meal. Every Sunday, we had a family barbecue at my nana's house where there were at least four grilled items on the table, and it was all meat—ribs, chicken, steak, and, for a little something extra, Nana would throw on some hot dogs.

But shortly after moving to the United States, I got my first job as a grocery store bagger. I was constantly and completely grossed out by the leaky packages of meat that I'd have to double bag so they wouldn't ooze onto other foods. That's when I made the decision to end my codependent relationship with animal products and go vegan.

I was also reading books and watching a lot of TV shows that were quickly drawing me into the American protest culture. One of the first books I read was *Animal Liberation* by Peter Singer. From there, I read all the books that Ingrid Newkirk and Carol J. Adams put out. I got so foot-stomping fired up that it made it easier to give up all the comfort food that I'd ever known. But mostly I was angry at myself. I couldn't believe I had spent my entire life eating meat and didn't really think about what I was doing for a single second.

It kind of spiraled out of control from there. I'm one of those hardheaded, all-or-nothing people. And when you're fourteen, you want to take everything to the limit, right? So, I just did it. Boom. No more meat or dairy for me. My parents were supportive, though knowing me, they probably thought they didn't have a choice, so they just went with it. Okay, so my mom was slightly annoyed at having to cook multiple dinners, but she quickly learned what to feed me. She bought me Tofurky and learned to make pumpkin pie with tofu. Mostly, I ate pasta for two years. I don't think I ate pasta again until I was in my midtwenties and it was my choice. But in 1995, there really wasn't a lot out there—the vegan alternatives were limited to rice milk, Boca burgers, and tofu.

The truth is, though, I was a vegan who didn't really have a taste for vegetables. I didn't eat a vegetable until I was like ten. I'm serious! My grandma would always put this big dish of ketchup-mayo sauce next to cucumbers because she knew I loved that sauce. But I didn't want to eat it on cucumbers. I honestly don't think I ate a green bean until I was twenty-five. I just started eating broccoli five years ago and I still have a hard time eating cauliflower.

And as long as I'm confessing, here's another one: Spam is still my favorite food. If I knew I were going to die tomorrow, I would go get some Spam. I haven't had it since I was twelve years old, but I remember that taste like it was yesterday. Guamanians eat the most Spam per capita because American troops brought this salty, tinned, ground-up mystery meat over during World War II. In Guam, there's a whole grocery store aisle dedicated to it—Guam Liberation Day Spam, Pimento Spam, Jalapeño Spam, and on and on. McDonald's serves Spam for breakfast.

I tell you this backstory because it drives our approach to veganism and the beginnings of the Herbivorous Butcher. For me, I didn't go vegan because I didn't like meat and dairy. I went vegan because I could no longer consume a creature or anything having to do with a creature. I still wanted to eat meat and sour cream and everything (especially Spam). And I eventually pushed Kale to become a vegan because I wanted my brother to be healthy and live forever. A couple of years later, when Kale and I first started selling our plant-based meat creations at the farmers' market, we heard stories from so many people and realized that they had pretty similar feelings about food. Our experience says humans become vegan for their own health and the health of the planet and all of its creatures, not because meat and dairy taste bad.

When we opened our shop in 2016, the Herbivorous Butcher sign definitively proclaimed a unique approach to veganism. Outside, there was a plaque dedicating our shop to the health of humans, animals, and the planet; inside, we put on traditional white butcher aprons and sold our goods in a big glass deli case. There are antique butcher knives hanging on the walls and welded into the legs of our standing counter. Even the front door handle is an antique cleaver. The fact is, we were the first vegan butchers in the world, and it was tough for some people to handle. People, that is, such as vegans. Even now we get emails about it: *I can't believe you did this.* A small group of vegans also say things like *When I hear the word* meat, *I get really sad.* Or *Instead of chicken, why not call it Thor's Thigh? Why not call it Porque?* Everyone is welcome to an opinion, but I say no one knows what Thor's Thigh tastes like, but they know what chicken tastes like.

We caught heat from the other side too. National pork and beef councils were writing slander pieces about us and getting their members all sizzled up. Butchers were sharpening their proverbial knives and coming after us because they felt we were mocking their craft. We actually got hate mail and death threats. Someone kept threatening to throw a pig's head through our front window. I mean, we had to set up a security system when we opened the shop just in case that pig's head was really going to come sailing through the glass— or worse.

But on the other side of it, so many vegans, vegetarians, and omnivores were thrilled about what we were doing. Thousands of folks felt like us—they simply missed a savory component on their plate along with the vegetable and starch. They wanted the protein without the fat and cholesterol. And we felt really good about bringing people together around the table again, eating the same thing, and having that sense of cohesion. It was a big deal to us.

And that brings me to this cookbook. There are a lot of plant-based meat options now, but people aren't sure how to cook with them, how to turn them into inventive dishes or standout meals. They don't understand that they can take any plant-based meat, whether it's our (*ahem,* clearly superior, small-batch) products or more mass-produced products, and use it in the exact same application that you would use a meat product. You can grill a vegan steak, or you can put it in the oven with a wine sauce, and if you do it right, it's going to be a savory, succulent masterpiece that just might fool your friends.

We were doing a lot of experimenting and making better and better meals for ourselves at home. We kept saying to each other, *Oh man, if everyone could eat these meals, they would know how good plant-based meats are and they would stop eating animals.* We just want everyone to know how good vegan food can actually be—and how possible it is for you to make your own meat-free meats at home. But the biggest reason that we started our business was to make positive changes in the world—for the health of people, animals, and the planet—and since we can't make enough food to feed everyone, we can at least share what we know with everyone and they can pass it on.

For me, the greatest surprise of all was seeing that our concept of a vegan butcher shop and high-quality mock meats were something that people wanted! When you're so passionate about a cause and the movement, it's hard to see the forest for the trees. We were so ingrained in every single little thing as we were opening the store—and I was so nervous that the public wouldn't get behind our mission. I was so wrong.

Meet Kale

Guamanian. Minnesotan. Kid brother. Molecular gastronomist. Herbivore.

I've been a vegan for ten years, since I was seventeen years old. My sister had been trying to convince me to stop eating meat for years, and she was strategic about it. I mean, she didn't send me videos of what happens in meat-packing facilities or cows being blown up. She knew I was trying to lose weight before I started college, and that was her hook. I was trying to avoid the "funny fat kid" trope that I felt I filled in high school. So she started peppering me with documentaries and articles and made me watch the movie *Forks Over Knives*. But, really, I could see with my own eyes that she had become a pretty healthy, happy plant eater.

So, I went cold turkey, so to speak. And it stuck. When I set my mind to something, I'm really good at seeing it through to the end. (It's a Walch family trait, apparently.) The bigger problem was getting my dad to accept it. It was heartbreaking, really. I was living with him back then, and we loved going around the country looking for the best burgers and ribs. We had ribs all over the place, from Kansas City to Memphis. I needed to convince him that I wouldn't have to sacrifice anything with this new diet because I was going to try to make products that are just as good or better than what we had. It took about a year and a half, but I finally came up with a recipe he would approve of—the Smoky House Rib (page 21). He began to see the merit of what we were doing. And he finally got over it.

In the beginning, Aubry and I weren't developing our recipes together all that much; we were both working on our recipes independently because we never had any intention of using them for anything. It was just making stuff we wanted to eat.

What we were attempting with our recipes wasn't really new. Making plant-based meats has been around since the 1970s. So, we started with basic recipes like those we found in *Vegan Vittles*. But they just didn't have the depth of flavor, that savory umami that I was missing, so we needed to re-create that wheel. It took hundreds of failed batches before I finally got the one that we still use today. I started to learn the principles behind making the meats and what role ingredients actually play in the final product.

It was after I dropped out of Bible college that we looked at all these recipes we had. And that's where we started collaborating and sharing the things that we learned as we were trying to capture the flavors of the foods we were missing so much. We could still feel like we were taking part in our culture—both the meat-loving Guamanian and meat-loving Midwesterner sides of our cultural experiences—it's just that the protein we use is different now. We can still have big holiday dinners; it's just that a few molecules are different.

We were grabbing drinks on Aubry's patio one evening when the light bulb popped on—it came about after my whole idea of becoming a pastor crashed and burned. Aubry had a nine-to-five job as a bookkeeper and had long had this dream of going into business with me. We thought about going into the restaurant business, but the failure rate was high. And that's when Aubry brought up the idea of a vegan butcher shop—and we laughed and drank some more and talked about what a ridiculous idea that was. We knew it hadn't been done. But, ultimately, we thought . . . *of course we should open a vegan butcher shop!* And we became determined like only a couple of strong-willed hardheads can be. We figured, even if we fail, it would be the first failure of its kind—and we were okay with that.

From there, we kicked it into gear. I was a server at the time, so I thought, *I'm going to save up all my tip money so that we can get a booth at the farmers' market and start selling this stuff.* We booked time at a community kitchen and started perfecting our recipes to make in larger batches. We had our friends and even strangers try the stuff to make sure we weren't crazy. Everybody confirmed it: Our meats were actually delicious. Not long after that, we got incorporated as a business. We did all that within a month from when we first had the idea.

We started with five products and secured a booth at the Minneapolis Farmers Market—one of the biggest and best in the country—and we began figuring out how to attract attention. Aubry worked the booth, and I was the sample guy. Attracting attention wasn't that hard for me. After I dropped out of Bible college, I let myself be myself for the first time ever and would buy the weirdest stuff I could find at Salvation Army to proclaim that fact. Prince was my inspiration for the wardrobe back then, if that gives you a picture.

We loved to psyche people out and pass off our creations as the real thing—actually, that was our favorite thing to do. We had a big sign that said meat-free meats. Sometimes I'd just stand in front of the first meat, and people would see just free meats. And they would try it and then they'd be like, *Is this venison? What kind of meat is this?* Even if they didn't buy anything, we achieved that "gotcha" moment, and that made it worth it for us. We were fine with tricking people into eating less meat—or going full vegan.

And we did develop a loyal clientele pretty quickly! A lot of our customers would challenge us to make their nana's Italian sausage or beer brats. Every week we would sell out, and people kept pushing us to do more and more, but we could do only so much out of the community kitchen. So, we did a Kickstarter campaign with the help of a social media manager. Around the same time, a very compassionate and forward-thinking investor approached us, a man who wanted to make our dreams of opening a vegan butcher shop come true. Between the Kickstarter and that kind gentleman, we opened the Herbivorous Butcher in 2016.

Obviously, a vegan butcher shop is an oxymoron. We figured it'd piss people off or they'd be really excited about it, but either way they'd tell someone. Our deviousness paid off. Haters aside, we now have a loyal—some say cultlike—following, and we ship all over the United States and Puerto Rico. Our first few months were pretty crazy: Guy Fieri roared in and put us on his show, and we even had Sir Paul McCartney's people call us up when he was in town for a concert and ask us to prepare a tray of plant-based meats, cheeses, and sandwiches for him.

(Okay, I'll tell you the Sir Paul story even though it represents one of the biggest regrets of our lives. He gave us backstage passes, and we were in this room waiting for him for a long time. And there was an open bar in there. And we were so nervous. We got plastered. Just plastered. And when it was finally time to meet him, we were like, *Oh God, we can't do this. We're so toasted. We screwed up.* I can't even remember what I said. I made a stupid joke or something and he didn't love it, but he was really nice, and he said, "I want to make sure that people in America see you as big of a deal as you are in England.")

So, there you have it. We're proud to be a part of promoting a plant-based diet, as when someone becomes vegan, the planet immediately breathes a little bit easier—literally! Deforestation and carbon emissions from the meat and dairy industry aren't doing the planet a lot of favors, so every day someone eats a vegan diet, it literally affects the Earth and contributes to a better future for us all.

Even more, we're happy to contribute to people's good health. Our products and the recipes that follow are all high in protein and low in fat. The vegan/vegetarian diet can be sometimes lacking in B_6 and B_{12} vitamins, if you're not careful about it, because they're usually found in meat. And all of our products provide those nutrients. A lot of our customers have to watch their cholesterol and reduce their meat consumption per doctor's orders, and we're more than excited about helping them reach those goals.

This cookbook helps us carry our mission forward; these are recipes that you can make in your own kitchen just as Aubry and I did, early on, in our tiny apartment kitchens. And you can make them using items you can get down the street at the grocery store, Asian market, or co-op. At the Herbivorous Butcher shop, we still handcraft our products in small batches using the best natural ingredients we can source. You just can't get the same flavor, texture, and versatility from the packaged items that come rolling off the factory belt from the big manufacturers—but you can get all that by making meat-free meats yourself!

For me, I hope you'll make and enjoy these recipes—and then make them your own. I'd love for you to experience the same feelings I had when I first started making them. Through the magic of food science, you can make fool-your-friends meat bases and then manipulate everything about the savory doughs, from the basic flavor to the texture to the way it's served. There are endless possibilities. Discovering that was so exciting to me, and I hope it will be for you too.

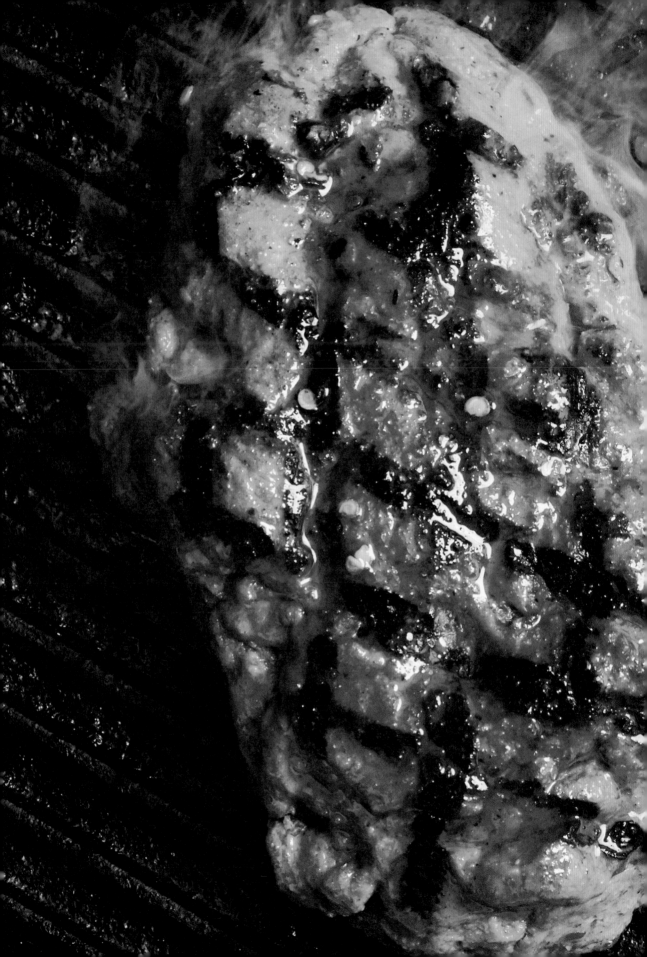

CHAPTER
1

Meat Made without Meat

Vegan butchery is a culinary art unlike any other. More alchemy than science, it has a lot more wiggle room for creative expression than you'll find in many cooking traditions. Growing up, I didn't cook a lot of meat because I was frustrated at the limitations; the most I could do to a cut of meat was marinate it and cook it well. As a vegan, I began experimenting with making plant-based meats and found a world of unlimited possibilities. Like some kind of mad (and hungry!) scientist, I discovered I could manipulate the flavor and texture of the meat at the molecular level at the very moment of its creation.

The recipes in this chapter are the original versions we perfected for friends and family years ago, popular recipes that we sold at the farmers' market and continue to sell at the Herbivorous Butcher. We're stoked to share them with you!

—Kale

The Rib

MAKES 2¾ LB [1.3 KG]

It's been said that a journey of a thousand miles begins with a single step. Well, my journey of a thousand vegan meats began with one rib. Before I went fully vegan in 2012, my father and I used to travel the country looking for the best burgers and ribs in every town we passed through. After I went vegan, I knew I needed a good rib to make sure I stayed vegan. After more than two hundred failed batches (and one attempt that filled my dad's house with hickory smoke that stuck to our dog and furniture for years), I finally made a batch that I was happy with. At the Herbivorous Butcher, that original recipe is the Smoky House Rib, and we still sell thousands of pounds of it every year. Presented for you here is a pared-down version of the recipe that will give you more flexibility and room for creativity. —*Kale*

For the Dry Mixture	
13 OZ [370 G]	VITAL WHEAT GLUTEN
⅓ CUP [20 G]	NUTRITIONAL YEAST FLAKES
2 TBSP	GARBANZO BEAN FLOUR
1 TBSP	ALL-PURPOSE FLOUR
2 TBSP	GRANULATED GARLIC
2 TBSP	ONION POWDER
1 TBSP	PAPRIKA
1 TBSP	SALT
For the Wet Mixture	
1¾ CUPS [420 ML]	APPLE JUICE
½ CUP [120 ML]	WATER
¼ CUP [60 ML]	SOY SAUCE
2 TBSP	LIQUID SMOKE
3 TBSP	BROWN SUGAR
2 TBSP	VEGETABLE OIL, FOR SEARING
For the Braising Broth	
⅓ CUP [80 ML]	BEEF BROTH CONCENTRATE [PAGE 199]
5 CUPS [1.2 L]	WATER

HOW TO MAKE IT

Preheat the oven to 325°F [165°C]. Grease a 9 by 13 in [23 by 33 cm] baking dish.

To make the dry mixture: In a large bowl, add the gluten, nutritional yeast, garbanzo bean flour, all-purpose flour, granulated garlic, onion powder, paprika, and salt. Stir well to combine.

To make the wet mixture: In a separate large bowl, add the apple juice, water, soy sauce, liquid smoke, and brown sugar. Whisk well to combine.

Slowly stir the wet mixture into the dry mixture. As the dough thickens, knead it by hand by placing it on a lightly floured surface and pressing it with the heel of the hand in a forward rolling motion. Rotate the dough and repeat for 1 to 2 minutes until no dry spots remain.

CONT'D

Transfer the dough to a large cutting board or clean surface. With a rolling pin, roll out the dough into a flat rectangle, about 1½ in [4 cm] thick. With a pizza cutter, cut out 4 to 5 in [10 to 12.5 cm] long rib-shaped pieces and set aside.

In a skillet or small sauté pan over medium-high heat, add the oil. Once heated, add the ribs and sear until they're golden brown, but not burnt, on both sides.

To make the broth: In a small bowl, whisk together the beef broth concentrate and water. (Try out the recipe as written first, but feel free to be creative here. Any barbecue sauce or marinade will work great; the ribs take on the flavor of whatever they're cooked in.)

Arrange your ribs in a single layer in the prepared baking dish, then pour on the braising broth (or chosen sauce), ensuring each one is almost completely covered. Cover the dish with foil and bake for 1 hour. Check to see if each piece is firm; add another 10 minutes if needed. Remove from the pan, store in an airtight container, and enjoy within a week.

Pro Tip

If you're planning to grill the ribs, let them cool overnight for best results. To make the rib recipe into a "rack" rather than individual ribs, simply leave the long rectangular shape intact when rolling out the dough and make small cuts between your desired ribs to imitate a rack shape. Grill as directed (see page 66), adding a few more minutes if necessary.

STEAMING EQUIPMENT

Steaming is one of the more efficient and consistent ways of cooking our vegan meats. But a steaming apparatus isn't a common item in the home cook's arsenal. When we first started doing test batches of our meats at home, we used a dim sum steamer, perhaps better known as a three-tier steamer pot. Tried and true, the dim sum steamer has never let us down; its elements keep ingredients sealed up tight, which is critical to a steaming process that cooks its contents evenly. *Bain-marie*, by the way, is a fancy French name for "water bath." It's basically a pot, bowl, or pan that is placed into another steamer pot to gently warm or cook the food inside.

The Butcher Burger

MAKES 8 TO 10 BURGERS

For those who have graduated to plant-based burgers but aren't always in the mood for the processed packaged patties found in grocery store aisles, may we present for your consideration the Butcher Burger. As with all the meats in this book, let this recipe be your base, a (mighty delicious) canvas on which you can paint a masterpiece of your own. Grill-tested and approved, this burger has been known to win over the most skeptical diner.

For the Dry Mixture	
3 CUPS [425 G]	VITAL WHEAT GLUTEN
2 CUPS [265 G]	GROUND SEITAN
¼ CUP [15 G]	NUTRITIONAL YEAST FLAKES
2 TBSP	GRANULATED GARLIC
2 TBSP	ONION POWDER
For the Wet Mixture	
2 CUPS [480 ML]	WATER
½ CUP [120 ML]	BEEF BROTH CONCENTRATE [PAGE 199]
3 TBSP	VEGETABLE OIL
3 TBSP	SOY SAUCE
1 TBSP	RED WINE VINEGAR

HOW TO MAKE IT

Prepare your steaming apparatus of choice (see page 22). Grease the inside of two bain-marie pots.

To make the dry mixture: In a large bowl, add the gluten, seitan, nutritional yeast, granulated garlic, and onion powder. Stir to combine.

To make the wet mixture: In a separate large bowl, add the water, broth concentrate, oil, soy sauce, and vinegar. Whisk together well.

Slowly stir the wet mixture into the dry mixture. Once the dough becomes too thick to stir, knead for 1 to 2 minutes until no dry spots remain. Divide the dough into two equal parts.

Place one piece of dough into each bain-marie pot, pressing the dough along the sides to eliminate excess air and flattening the top as well as you can. Place a piece of foil over each pan and seal tightly. Put the pots into your steaming apparatus and steam for 1½ hours.

CONT'D

Remove the pans from the steaming apparatus and let cool for a bit before removing the burgers. For optimal slicing, let cool overnight. Slice as thin or thick as you'd like, pan-fry, grill, or store in an airtight container in the refrigerator, and enjoy within a week.

GOTTA HAVE IT: NUTRITIONAL YEAST

In all the meat recipes in this volume, you'll find nutritional yeast—an ingredient rich in umami peptides and B vitamins that, along with the garlic and onion powders, makes a complete savory experience. Some recipes incorporate ingredients that are rich in the umami peptides but also impart other flavors—tomato juice, for example, is umami and rich in iron and is thus used in "beef" recipes to impart a more realistic flavor. The Beef Broth Concentrate (page 199) in our recipes is an umami powerhouse, full of soy sauce, nutritional yeast, and herbs and spices that enhance the umami flavors even further. Our Chicken Broth Powder (page 200) creates a more complex and complete savory profile, utilizing herbs and spices as well as onion powder and nutritional yeast to create a rich, well-rounded broth base.

Porterhouse Steak

MAKES 3 LB [1.4 KG]

At the end of a long day of vegan butchery, am I always in the mood to make a whole feast? That's a hard no. But is there always gas left in the tank to at least fry up a juicy steak along with whatever rice I have handy? Oh yeah. And for about a year or two of my life that's exactly what I did, every night. May it serve you as well as it has served me. —*Kale*

For the Braising Broth	
9 CUPS [2.1 L]	WATER
¼ CUP [60 ML]	BEEF BROTH CONCENTRATE [PAGE 199]
2 TBSP	SOY SAUCE
½ CUP [120 ML]	TOMATO JUICE
For the Dry Mixture	
15 OZ [430 G]	VITAL WHEAT GLUTEN
¼ CUP [15 G]	NUTRITIONAL YEAST FLAKES
2 TBSP	GARBANZO BEAN FLOUR
2 TBSP	RED BEET POWDER
1 TBSP	GRANULATED GARLIC
1 TBSP	ONION POWDER
1 TBSP	SMOKED PAPRIKA
1 TBSP	SALT
For the Wet Mixture	
¾ CUP [180 ML]	TOMATO JUICE
¾ CUP [180 ML]	APPLE JUICE
¾ CUP [180 ML]	WATER
¼ CUP [65 G]	TOMATO PASTE
¼ CUP [60 ML]	VEGETABLE OIL
2 TBSP	SOY SAUCE
1 TBSP	LIQUID SMOKE

HOW TO MAKE IT
Preheat the oven to 325°F [165°C]. Grease a baking sheet or line it with parchment paper.

To make the braising broth: In a large pot, combine the water, broth concentrate, soy sauce, and tomato juice. Bring to a slow boil while preparing the wet and dry mixtures.

To make the dry mixture: In a large bowl, combine the gluten, nutritional yeast, garbanzo bean flour, beet powder, granulated garlic, onion powder, smoked paprika, and salt. Stir well.

To make the wet mixture: In a separate large bowl, combine the tomato juice, apple juice, water, tomato paste, oil, soy sauce, and liquid smoke. Whisk well.

Slowly stir the wet mixture into the dry mixture. When the dough becomes sinewy, knead it by hand until no dry spots remain.

Transfer the dough to a large cutting board or clean surface. Using a serrated knife, carve off 8 oz [230 g] pieces. Knead each piece over itself and flatten into a "steak" shape.

Place the steaks on the prepared baking sheet and bake for 15 minutes.

Remove the steaks from the oven and carefully place into the braising broth, turn the heat to medium-low, and simmer for 25 minutes.

From here you can pan-fry the steaks with a little olive oil or let cool overnight to use in other recipes. Store any remaining portion in an airtight container in the refrigerator and enjoy within a week.

Big Ole Beefy Beef

MAKES 3 LB [1.4 KG]

They say necessity breeds invention. Such was the case with this popular dish. Minnesotans are a hearty bunch, but behind that stoic resistance to the bitter winter cold is an arsenal of soul-warming recipes that get us through. In our first year in business, the people demanded such sustenance from us. So, I set out to make a pot roast delicious enough to warm even a snowman's heart. But what I created could not fairly be just a pot roast—oh no! It was too sumptuous, too momentous, too beefy to just be a pot roast. Thus, when this recipe was born, Aubry dubbed it Big Ole Beefy Beef. —*Kale*

For the Dry Mixture	
2½ CUPS [355 G]	VITAL WHEAT GLUTEN
½ CUP [35 G]	NUTRITIONAL YEAST FLAKES
2 TBSP	RED BEET POWDER
2 TBSP	ONION POWDER
2 TBSP	GRANULATED GARLIC
2 TBSP	MUSHROOM POWDER
2 TBSP	TAPIOCA POWDER
For the Wet Mixture	
1¼ CUPS [300 ML]	WATER
¼ CUP [60 ML]	SOY SAUCE
¼ CUP [60 ML]	BEEF BROTH CONCENTRATE [PAGE 199]
3 TBSP	ROBUST RED WINE (SUCH AS A ZINFANDEL)
2 TBSP	RED WINE VINEGAR
2 TBSP	VEGETABLE OIL
2 TSP	LIQUID SMOKE
For the "Beast's Bath"	
¼ CUP [60 ML]	OLIVE OIL
3 MEDIUM	CARROTS, PEELED AND SLICED
2 MEDIUM	YELLOW ONIONS, THICKLY SLICED
¼ CUP [60 ML]	BEEF BROTH CONCENTRATE [PAGE 199]
1½ CUPS [360 ML]	ROBUST RED WINE (SUCH AS A ZINFANDEL)
1½ CUPS [360 ML]	WATER
3 SPRIGS	FRESH PARSLEY
3 SPRIGS	FRESH THYME
6	BAY LEAVES

HOW TO MAKE IT

Preheat the oven to 275°F [135°C].

To make the dry mixture: In a large bowl, add the gluten, nutritional yeast, beet powder, onion powder, granulated garlic, mushroom powder, and tapioca powder and stir to combine.

To make the wet mixture: In another large bowl, add the water, soy sauce, and broth concentrate and whisk well. Add the red wine, vinegar, oil, and liquid smoke. Whisk to combine.

Slowly stir the wet mixture into the dry mixture. Once the dough becomes too thick to stir, knead until no dry spots remain. You might need to do this for a while, so don't give up! Let the dough rest for 20 to 30 minutes.

Meanwhile, to make the "Beast's Bath": In a Dutch oven or large pot over high heat, heat the olive oil. Add the carrots, stir for 1 minute, then add the onions. Stir occasionally to avoid burning, for about 10 minutes, until the vegetables start to caramelize. Set the vegetables aside. In a small bowl or

CONT'D

measuring cup, combine the broth concentrate, red wine, and water. If using a Dutch oven, pour in a small amount of the liquid to deglaze, stirring to scrape up the browned bits from the bottom and reserve to add later with the broth.

Knead your dough a few times, then form into a rectangle shape. Add a bit more oil to the Dutch oven or pan, then carefully sear both sides of the roast.

Pour the rest of the prepared "Beast's Bath" over the seared roast, then surround with the carrots and onions. Arrange the parsley, thyme, and bay leaves on and around the roast.

Put the lid on your Dutch oven, or cover the pan with foil, then place in the oven for 2½ hours. Let cool, then re-cover the pan with foil, store in the refrigerator, and enjoy within 1 week.

Extra Credit

If you plan on eating your roast right away, all the power to you! The roast and root veggies will be quite tender and perfect. *But*, if you're in the mood for something crazy and want to try the most succulent gravy you'll ever taste, remove the roast and herbs from the pan, and put the remaining vegetables into a blender with just a splash of wine. Process until smooth and pour it over everything you can see.

Pro Tip

If ever you received a Dutch oven as a present and tucked it away behind the island of misfit kitchen tools, it's time to bring it out into the light. If not, a classic 9 by 13 in [23 by 33 cm] baking dish will work just fine.

Ground Beef

MAKES 1 LB [455 G]

Fully cooked and ready to put in any recipe in about an hour, the ground beef is a jack-of-all-trades. It's fresher and more customizable than store-bought alternatives, and I always have some in my refrigerator to use throughout the week. —*Kale*

1 TBSP	SOY SAUCE
1 TBSP	BEEF BROTH CONCENTRATE [PAGE 199]
1 CUP [145 G]	VITAL WHEAT GLUTEN
1 TBSP	NUTRITIONAL YEAST FLAKES
1 TSP	GRANULATED GARLIC
1 TSP	ONION POWDER
⅓ CUP [80 ML]	TOMATO JUICE
¼ CUP [60 ML]	WATER
2 TSP	VEGETABLE OIL

SAVORY THOUGHTS

It took science millennia to crack the code on the taste and feeling of "savory." As ridiculous as it may seem, if you try to describe the sensation of "savory," it's rather difficult to do. It's not quite salty, not quite sweet, but rather a rich, sumptuous flavor that we are biologically designed to love and crave. Scientists believe that the perception of savory in a particular food points to the presence of proteins and amino acids. Only recently was it found that what we call "savory" is actually a two-part experience: umami and the lesser-known sibling kokumi. Umami is the perception of glutamates (one type of amino acid) in food, while kokumi is the sense of richness, body, and complexity. In many of our plant-based meat recipes, for example, you'll find onions and garlic. These are rich in glutamates and "kokumi-rich" peptides that enhance the flavors around them, boosting the perception of sweet, salty, and umami flavors.

HOW TO MAKE IT

Bring a large pot of salted water to a boil. Add the soy sauce and broth concentrate.

In a large bowl, mix together the gluten, nutritional yeast, granulated garlic, and onion powder. Set aside. In a separate large bowl, whisk together the tomato juice, water, and oil; slowly add to the dry ingredients while stirring.

Mix until the dough begins to come together, then knead by hand until no dry spots remain. Divide the dough into two portions and knead a few more times before submerging in the boiling water.

Bring to a boil again and immediately lower the heat to a simmer. Simmer for 45 minutes, until firm.

Remove the beef from the pot and let cool for a few minutes. Chop the beef into manageable chunks. In a food processor or stand mixer, process the chunks in batches until well ground.

The beef is ready to use immediately in any recipe that calls for it. Store any unused portion in an airtight container in the refrigerator and consume within 1 week.

Pork Chops

MAKES 5 OR 6 CHOPS

Our dad would make great shake-and-bake pork chops—they were so good, in fact, that our small ears would perk up at the mere sound of a paper bag crumpling. We just had to relive those days by re-creating a bit of that magic in vegan form—and it all started with this chop. See if you don't get nostalgic too.

For the Dry Mixture	
2 CUPS [285 G]	VITAL WHEAT GLUTEN
⅓ CUP [20 G]	NUTRITIONAL YEAST FLAKES
2 TBSP	TAPIOCA FLOUR
2 TSP	CHICKEN BROTH POWDER [PAGE 200]
2 TSP	ONION POWDER
2 TSP	GRANULATED GARLIC
For the Wet Mixture	
1 BLOCK [400 G]	FIRM TOFU, CRUMBLED
1 CUP [240 ML]	WATER
½ CUP [120 ML]	PULP-FREE ORANGE JUICE
¼ CUP [60 ML]	VEGETABLE OIL
2 TBSP	TAHINI
2 TSP	WHITE MISO
1 TSP	SALT
1 TSP	GROUND FENNEL
½ TSP	GROUND BASIL
½ TSP	DRIED ROSEMARY
	OLIVE OIL, FOR DRIZZLING
2 QT [2 L]	WATER
¼ CUP [60 ML]	SOY SAUCE
	SALT
	FRESHLY GROUND BLACK PEPPER

HOW TO MAKE IT

Preheat the oven to 325°F [165°C]. Line a baking sheet with parchment paper or spray it with nonstick cooking spray.

To make the dry mixture: In a large bowl, combine the gluten, nutritional yeast, tapioca flour, broth powder, onion powder, and granulated garlic. Set aside.

To make the wet mixture: In a blender or food processor, combine the tofu, water, orange juice, vegetable oil, tahini, miso, salt, fennel, basil, and rosemary. Process until smooth, making sure to scrape down the sides so no chunks remain.

Pour the blender contents into the dry mixture. Stir until the dough comes together, then knead until no dry spots remain.

Transfer the dough to a large cutting board or clean surface. With a serrated knife, carve off 7 oz [200 g] pieces.

Knead each piece over itself a few times, then form into the desired shape. We form ours by stretching one side into a "chop" shape.

Put the chops on the prepared baking sheet and drizzle with a little olive oil. Bake for 25 minutes.

CONT'D

In a large pot, bring the water to a boil. Add the soy sauce and a pinch each of salt and pepper.

Remove the chops from the oven and carefully transfer each piece to the pot. Bring to a boil, then quickly lower the heat to a simmer for 20 minutes.

Remove the chops from the boiling broth and let cool. The chops are ready to be pan-fried but can also be cooled overnight to improve the texture for use in other recipes. Store in an airtight container in the refrigerator and consume within 1 week.

TAPIOCA FLOUR = TEXTURE

Vegan meats can be manipulated in just about any way, and every new ingredient adds a new dimension to the finished product. Starches are master manipulators, and one of our favorites is tapioca flour, a starch that improves the texture of the finished product by increasing the moisture retention of the meat. With meats like the Pork Chop (page 35) that cook in a savory broth, this not only helps the finished texture but allows the chop to preserve much more of the broth's flavor as well. Play around with different ratios and see what else you discover!

Chicken Cutlets

MAKES 3 LB [1.4 KG]

This recipe was a long time in the making. It came about because Aubry was longing for the Sizzler's Malibu Chicken that she loved so much as a kid on Guam. So, like many of our recipes, the Chicken Cutlet was first made as a gift, a cash-strapped attempt to make a birthday present for Aubry better than anything money could buy. Obviously, it was imperative I get it right. Since then, this recipe has traveled with us to food festivals all around the country. It's time we all share in the sizzle. —*Kale*

For the Dry Mixture	
3 CUPS [425 G]	VITAL WHEAT GLUTEN
⅓ CUP [20 G]	NUTRITIONAL YEAST FLAKES
3 TBSP	ALL-PURPOSE FLOUR
1 TBSP	GARBANZO BEAN FLOUR
2 TBSP	ONION POWDER
2 TBSP	GRANULATED GARLIC
2 TBSP	CHICKEN BROTH POWDER [PAGE 200]
For the Wet Mixture	
1½ CUPS [360 ML]	WATER
1 CUP [240 ML]	UNSWEETENED NONDAIRY MILK
3 TBSP	VEGETABLE OIL
2 TBSP	WHITE MISO PASTE
1 TBSP	SALT

HOW TO MAKE IT

Fill a large pot with about 3 qt [2.7 L] of water, making sure it's not too full, and bring to a boil.

To make the dry mixture: In a large bowl, add the gluten, nutritional yeast, all-purpose flour, garbanzo bean flour, onion powder, granulated garlic, and broth powder; stir to combine.

To make the wet mixture: In a separate large bowl, add the water, nondairy milk, oil, miso, and salt and whisk well, ensuring that the miso is thoroughly combined.

Gradually pour the wet mixture into the dry mixture, stirring with a spoon until the dough becomes too thick to stir. Use your hands to knead the dough in the bowl until few or no dry spots remain visible.

Transfer the dough to a large cutting board or clean surface. With a serrated knife, carve off pieces 2 to 2½ oz [55 to 70 g] in weight.

Knead each piece over itself several times and stretch one side to resemble a flat "drumstick" shape.

CONT'D

Drop the pieces of chicken into the boiling water, then lower the heat to medium. Simmer the chicken for 35 minutes. Don't let the water reach a full boil. Stir gently occasionally to prevent sticking.

After 35 minutes, drain the pot into a colander and let the cutlets cool for a bit. They *can* be used for another recipe immediately, but the texture benefits from sitting in the fridge for a few hours or overnight if you have time.

Store cutlets in an airtight container in the refrigerator and consume within 1 week.

Pro Tip

The more times the dough is kneaded over itself, the firmer the finished texture will be.

SEITAN 101

It's pronounced *SAY-tan*, but what the devil is it?

What it is:
We've heard it called "wheat meat," which is a pretty apt description. When you cook up a batch, it's a real faker, taking on the look and texture of meat. That's why it's a popular meat substitute for vegetarians and vegans. All of our plant-based meat recipes are considered seitan.

How it tastes:
Seitan has a savory taste, probably closest to unseasoned chicken or a portobello mushroom. But it's pretty bland without some dolling up. (That's where we come in.) The reason it's popular is more of a texture thing—soy-based tofu or tempeh just doesn't have the same structure.

Why make it:
You can buy prepared seitan, but a box of it at your local market might make your wallet hurt. Besides, ours is way better and it's easy to make. It starts with vital wheat gluten, a product made by rinsing away the starch in the wheat dough, leaving just the high-protein gluten behind.

How to make it:
Seitan is often a fickle thing, and doesn't like to be rushed; when cooking seitan, we must be careful to monitor its temperature. Boiling seitan dough for a prolonged time will result in a tough yet porous meat that isn't very realistic or appealing. This principle applies also to cooking a completed recipe—grilling and pan-frying at a low temperature for a longer time will always give you a better result.

Pepperoni

MAKES 2¼ LB [1 KG]

One of our "starting five," our pepperoni has been with us since our first day at the farmers' market. If you've ever been curious about smoking or curing vegan meats, this is a good place to start—the texture and flavor can be changed dramatically with little effort.

For the Dry Mixture	
12 OZ [340 G]	VITAL WHEAT GLUTEN
⅓ CUP [20 G]	NUTRITIONAL YEAST FLAKES
1½ TBSP	TAPIOCA FLOUR
1 TBSP	PAPRIKA
1 TBSP	RED BEET POWDER
1 TBSP	CRUSHED PEPPERCORN MÉLANGE
½ TBSP	FENNEL SEED, CRUSHED
½ TBSP	RED PEPPER FLAKES
½ TBSP	SALT
¾ TSP	GROUND CUMIN
¾ TSP	GROUND MUSTARD
½ TSP	ONION POWDER
¼ TSP	CAYENNE PEPPER
For the Wet Mixture	
1½ CUPS [360 ML]	TOMATO JUICE
½ CUP [120 ML]	VEGETABLE OIL
⅓ CUP [75 G]	TOMATO PASTE
¼ CUP [60 ML]	WATER
¼ CUP [60 ML]	SOY SAUCE
1½ TBSP	WHITE MISO PASTE
2	GARLIC CLOVES, MINCED

HOW TO MAKE IT

Prepare your steaming apparatus of choice (see page 22). Tear off two 12 in [30 cm] pieces of aluminum foil.

To make the dry mixture: In a large bowl, mix together the gluten, nutritional yeast, tapioca flour, paprika, beet powder, peppercorns, fennel seed, red pepper flakes, salt, cumin, mustard, onion powder, and cayenne, ensuring that the fennel and peppercorns are well crushed in a spice grinder or mortar and pestle but not ground into a powder.

To make the wet mixture: In a separate large bowl, add the tomato juice, oil, tomato paste, water, soy sauce, miso, and garlic. Whisk together well.

Slowly pour the wet mixture into the dry mixture and stir until the dough thickens. Knead the pepperoni for 1 to 2 minutes until no dry spots remain.

Transfer the dough to a large cutting board or clean surface and divide into two 1 lb [455 g] portions.

CONT'D

Using your hands, roll and work the dough into long logs just shorter than the width of the foil. Place the long pepperoni logs onto the foil and roll up tight, twisting tightly at the ends.

Put the encased pepperoni logs into the steaming apparatus and steam for 1 hour.

Let cool overnight before slicing to your desired width. Store in an airtight container in the refrigerator and enjoy within 1 week.

Milano Salami

MAKES 3 LB [1.4 KG]

This recipe came about as a customer request back during our farmers' market days. She wanted us to make a vegan version of her grandma's favorite Italian sandwich. Seriously, how could we resist? Besides, we're always up for a good challenge. The result might even have fooled Nonna.

For the Dry Mixture	
3 CUPS [425 G]	VITAL WHEAT GLUTEN
½ CUP [35 G]	NUTRITIONAL YEAST FLAKES
1 TBSP	ALL-PURPOSE FLOUR
1 TBSP	WHITE PEPPER
2 TSP	RED BEET POWDER
2 TBSP	GRANULATED GARLIC
2 TBSP	ONION POWDER
For the Wet Mixture	
¾ CUP [180 ML]	TOMATO JUICE
¾ CUP [180 ML]	APPLE JUICE
½ CUP [120 ML]	OLIVE OIL
6 TBSP [100 G]	TOMATO PASTE
1 TBSP	SOY SAUCE
3 TBSP	WHITE MISO PASTE
2 TBSP	WHITE WINE VINEGAR
2 TSP	DRIED MARJORAM
1 TSP	DRIED THYME
1 TSP	DRIED BASIL
8 OZ [225 G]	EXTRA-FIRM TOFU
5	GARLIC CLOVES, MINCED

HOW TO MAKE IT

Prepare your steaming apparatus of choice (see page 22). Tear three large pieces of aluminum foil no wider than the bain-marie pot or basket of your steamer.

To make the dry mixture: In a large bowl, mix together the gluten, nutritional yeast, flour, white pepper, beet powder, granulated garlic, and onion powder. Set aside.

To make the wet mixture: In a food processor or blender, add the tomato juice, apple juice, oil, tomato paste, soy sauce, miso, vinegar, marjoram, thyme, and basil. Blend until smooth. Add the tofu and pulse until flecks are still visible but no large chunks remain. Add the minced garlic to the mixture.

Add the wet mixture to the dry mixture and stir to combine. Once it gets too thick to stir, use your hands to knead it until no dry spots are visible.

Transfer the dough to a large cutting board or clean surface. Use a serrated knife to cut the dough into three equal pieces. Knead and roll the individual pieces of dough into thin logs just shorter than the foil. Position a log on the bottom portion of a foil sheet. Tightly roll in foil, ensuring there are no tears. Repeat with the remaining logs and foil.

Steam the salami for 1 hour, then remove them from the steaming apparatus. Refrigerate overnight in an airtight container, slice thinly, and enjoy within a week.

Chamorro Chorizo

SERVES 2 TO 4

When I was a kid, I loved when I could tag along with my dad to his business breakfasts. It's probably where my entrepreneurial spirit was born—well, and my love for chorizo, of course. This recipe pays homage to the chorizo sausage they served at the Take Five Coffee Shop on Guam. It's decadent and salty, and if we do say so ourselves, it boasts a splendid combination of perfectly proportioned spices. —*Aubry*

1 LB [455 G]	GROUND BEEF [PAGE 33] OR OTHER GROUND BEEF CRUMBLES OR TOFU
1	YELLOW ONION, FINELY CHOPPED
⅓ CUP [80 ML]	WATER
¼ CUP [60 ML]	VEGETABLE OIL, PLUS MORE FOR FRYING
3 TBSP	APPLE CIDER VINEGAR
2	GARLIC CLOVES, CHOPPED
1 TBSP	ACHIOTE POWDER
2 TSP	CAYENNE PEPPER
1 TSP	SMOKED PAPRIKA
1 TSP	PAPRIKA
1 TSP	SALT
1 TSP	RED PEPPER FLAKES

HOW TO MAKE IT

In a large mixing bowl, add the beef, onion, water, oil, vinegar, garlic, achiote powder, cayenne, smoked paprika, paprika, salt, and red pepper flakes. Mix by hand until it's completely combined.

In a large skillet, heat the oil over medium heat and cook the chorizo mixture until browned and to your level of doneness. (We like to cook ours until it's crispy just around the edges.)

Enjoy with a rice and tofu scramble or a vegan-egg scramble. You can also make some killer tacos or nachos. Store in an airtight container in the refrigerator and enjoy within 1 week.

Deli Bologna

MAKES 1 LB [455 G]

Early in life, my dad taught me that a bologna sandwich with mayonnaise, ketchup, a little celery salt, and club crackers was just about all you needed. Bologna was, therefore, one of my first projects after I went vegan—and one of the first five items we ever sold at the Herbivorous Butcher. It had quite the cult following in our early days. We've since retired it in the store, but we'd like to bestow it upon you in all its sweet, tasty glory. —*Kale*

½ CUP [70 G]	VITAL WHEAT GLUTEN
¼ CUP [15 G]	NUTRITIONAL YEAST FLAKES
1 BLOCK [400 G]	EXTRA-FIRM TOFU
⅓ CUP [30 G]	AGAR-AGAR POWDER OR KONJAC POWDER
½ CUP [120 G]	TOMATO JUICE
¼ CUP [60 ML]	BEEF BROTH CONCENTRATE [PAGE 199]
2 TBSP	RED BEET POWDER
2 TBSP	VEGETABLE OIL
1 TSP	PAPRIKA
1 TSP	LIQUID SMOKE
2 TSP	SALT
2 TSP	ONION POWDER
2 TSP	GRANULATED GARLIC
1 TBSP	WHITE MISO PASTE
1 TBSP	MIRIN
1 TSP	CELERY SEED

HOW TO MAKE IT

Prepare your steaming apparatus of choice (see page 22). Grease a bain-marie pan.

In a large bowl, mix together the gluten and nutritional yeast. Set aside. Crumble the tofu into a blender. Add the agar-agar powder, tomato juice, broth concentrate, beet powder, oil, paprika, liquid smoke, salt, onion powder, granulated garlic, miso, mirin, and celery seed. Blend until smooth, scraping the sides as needed. Empty the blender contents into the bowl of dry ingredients. Stir until thoroughly combined, using your hands if necessary.

Put the bologna into the bain-marie pan. Cover with parchment paper, then foil. Steam for 50 minutes, then check to see if it's firm, adding a few more minutes if necessary.

Let cool in an airtight container in the refrigerator overnight, then slice thinly on a countertop meat slicer or by hand. Store in an airtight container in the refrigerator and enjoy within 1 week.

Pro Tip

If you can't find agar-agar powder or konjac powder at your local grocery store, give an Asian market a shot. If they don't have any either, don't sweat it, just add another ¼ cup [35 g] of gluten.

The Brat

MAKES 10 BRATS

Our journey of a million brats began with just one: the Italian. Since then, and often in collaboration with our customers, we've made more than fifty different kinds and the list keeps growing. Throw (just about) anything into this base recipe and make some magic of your own!

For the Dry Mixture	
2 CUPS [285 G]	VITAL WHEAT GLUTEN
⅓ CUP [20 G]	NUTRITIONAL YEAST FLAKES
2 TBSP	RED BEET POWDER
1 TSP	PAPRIKA
1 TSP	SMOKED PAPRIKA
1 TSP	BLACK PEPPER
1 TSP	ONION POWDER
1 TSP	GRANULATED GARLIC
For the Wet Mixture	
1½ CUPS [360 ML]	WATER
⅓ CUP [75 G]	MASHED CANNELLINI [WHITE KIDNEY] BEANS
2 TBSP	BEEF BROTH CONCENTRATE [PAGE 199]
2 TBSP	OLIVE OIL
2 TBSP	SOY SAUCE
1 TSP	LIQUID SMOKE

Extra Credit

For a Thai curry Brat, add Thai curry paste to the liquid ingredients and serve with pickled carrot, cilantro, and sweet chile sauce.

For a beer Brat, replace 1 cup [240 ml] of the water with a (flat*) beer of your choice and add a pinch of caraway seeds. *Caution! Make sure the beer is flat to avoid steaming explosions. (Please don't ask us how we know.)

HOW TO MAKE IT

Prepare your steaming apparatus of choice (see page 22). Tear off ten 8 in [20 cm] pieces of foil.

To make the dry mixture: In a large bowl, combine the gluten, nutritional yeast, beet powder, paprika, smoked paprikà, pepper, onion powder, and granulated garlic. Stir until well combined.

To make the wet mixture: In a medium bowl, combine the water, cannellini beans, broth concentrate, oil, soy sauce, and liquid smoke. Whisk well to combine.

Slowly add the wet mixture to the dry mixture and stir, kneading with your hands, if necessary, until no dry spots remain.

Divide the dough into level ⅓ cup [80 g] portions. You should have about ten portions. Form each portion into a brat shape and place on one end of each piece of foil. Roll up and twist the ends shut, like a wrapped candy.

Place the wrapped brats in the steamer and steam for 30 minutes. Check to ensure each brat is firm to the touch, adding more time if necessary. Let cool before unwrapping.

Sham

MAKES 1½ LB [680 G]

Did you know Guamanians eat more Spam per capita than any other country? This is thanks to the diets of the American troops who liberated the island during World War II. We even have our own special-edition "Guam Liberation Day" can of Spam on the island! For years, Aubry demanded a vegan Spam from me with little success. Until . . . —*Kale*

½ CUP [70 G]	VITAL WHEAT GLUTEN
¼ CUP [15 G]	NUTRITIONAL YEAST
¼ CUP [50 G]	CHICKEN BROTH POWDER [PAGE 200]
¼ CUP [25 G]	AGAR-AGAR POWDER OR KONJAC POWDER
1 BLOCK [400 G]	EXTRA-FIRM TOFU
½ CUP [120 ML]	WATER
¼ CUP [60 ML]	BEEF BROTH CONCENTRATE [PAGE 199]
2 TBSP	VEGETABLE OIL
2 TBSP	RED BEET POWDER
1 TBSP	WHITE MISO PASTE
1 TBSP	SUGAR
2 TSP	SALT
1 TSP	PAPRIKA
1 TSP	LIQUID SMOKE
1 TSP	ONION POWDER
1 TSP	GRANULATED GARLIC

HOW TO MAKE IT

Prepare your steaming apparatus of choice (see page 22). Grease two bain-marie pans.

In a large bowl, mix together the gluten, nutritional yeast, broth powder, and agar-agar powder. Set aside. In a blender, crumble the tofu, then add the water, broth concentrate, oil, beet powder, miso, sugar, salt, paprika, liquid smoke, onion powder, and granulated garlic. Blend until smooth. Empty the blender contents into the bowl of dry ingredients, scraping the sides with a spatula. Stir until thoroughly combined.

Use your hands to divide the mixture in half and put half of the mixture in each bain-marie pan. Cover with foil. Steam for 30 minutes, then check to see if the mixture is firm. Add a few more minutes if needed.

Let cool, then slice in half to make two semi-circles. Is it the exact shape of Spam? No, but it's a damn good luncheon meat. Store in an airtight container in the refrigerator and enjoy within 1 week.

Faux Gras

SERVES 6 TO 8

Keep that pinky up when making this recipe because we're venturing into Fancy Land. A much tastier (and leagues more ethical) version of the foie gras enjoyed by Brooklyn hipsters and gourmand wannabes the world over, this faux gras will prove to your friends: "Hey, I can be fancy and not be an a-hole!"

½ CUP [70 G]	SHELLED PECANS
½ CUP [70 G]	CASHEWS
¼ CUP [60 G]	HAZELNUTS
2 TBSP	BETTER BUTTER [PAGE 208]
2 CUPS [180 G]	CHOPPED SHIITAKE MUSHROOMS
½ LARGE [140 G]	YELLOW ONION, FINELY CHOPPED
2	GARLIC CLOVES, MINCED
¼ CUP [55 G]	REFINED COCONUT OIL
¼ CUP [50 G]	CHICKEN BROTH POWDER [PAGE 200]
3 TBSP	COGNAC
2 TBSP	SOY SAUCE
2 TBSP	FRESHLY SQUEEZED LEMON JUICE
2 TBSP	AGAR-AGAR POWDER
1 TBSP	WHITE MISO PASTE
1 TSP	TRUFFLE OIL
	SALT

HOW TO MAKE IT

Soak the pecans, cashews, and hazelnuts in water to cover overnight. If you're short on time, boil water, remove from the heat, and submerge the nuts in the hot water for a few hours. Drain the water before use.

In a small sauté pan over medium-high heat, melt the vegan butter. Add the mushrooms, onion, and garlic, and cook until the onions are translucent, about 4 minutes. Add the coconut oil to the pan and melt. Scrape the onion mixture into a food processor or blender and add the soaked nuts, broth powder, cognac, soy sauce, lemon juice, agar-agar powder, miso, and truffle oil and season with salt. Blend until smooth, scraping the sides as necessary, until no large pieces remain.

Lay out two large pieces of parchment paper. Use a spatula to scrape equal amounts of the blender contents onto the bottom half of each piece. Use the spatula to smooth out each portion into a log shape. Slowly roll each portion up like a tootsie roll, trying to avoid wrinkles in the parchment paper if possible, as the mixture will set in

CONT'D

this shape. Put each roll into the refrigerator overnight to set.

Unroll, slice or spread onto baguette or crackers, and enjoy! Store in an airtight container in the refrigerator for up to 1 week.

LET THIS GEL

You don't even want to know what's in gelatin. (Okay—and we cringe to tell you this—it's made from boiled animal parts.) The vegan substitute is agar-agar powder, a gelling, emulsifying agent made from seaweed. It creates a strong, thermally irreversible gel that sets at 85 to 90°F [30 to 32°C]. It works in this recipe and others by holding the ingredients together when the warm contents of the sauté pan are added to the blender.

Fish Sticks

MAKES 1.1 LB [510 G]

It's confession time, so lean a little closer. Even though we were both born on the island of Guam, we don't swim, and we've never really eaten fish. We even have cousins who were Olympic swimmers, so we're not sure what happened. Our mom tried to get Kale to eat fillet of fish sandwiches by telling him it was chicken, until she was busted. But faux fish, now that's a different story.

Start with	
2 BLOCKS [800 G]	FIRM TOFU
For the Marinade	
¼ CUP [60 ML]	LOW-SODIUM SOY SAUCE (WE PREFER KIMLAN)
2 TBSP	NUTRITIONAL YEAST FLAKES
2 TBSP	KELP GRANULES
2 TBSP	FRESHLY SQUEEZED LEMON JUICE
2 TBSP	VEGETABLE OIL
1 TSP	ONION POWDER
For the Breading	
½ CUP [70 G]	ALL-PURPOSE FLOUR
2 TBSP	CORNSTARCH
½ CUP [120 ML]	UNSWEETENED SOY MILK
1 TBSP	APPLE CIDER VINEGAR
¾ CUP [45 G]	PANKO BREAD CRUMBS
2 TBSP	NUTRITIONAL YEAST FLAKES
1 TSP	SALT
1 TSP	ONION POWDER
1 TSP	GRANULATED GARLIC
1 TSP	PAPRIKA
1 TSP	DRIED PARSLEY
3 CUPS [720 ML]	VEGETABLE OIL
	VEGAN TARTAR SAUCE, FOR SERVING

HOW TO MAKE IT

Wrap the tofu in several layers of paper towels. Stack a cutting board and a light weight of some kind on top of the tofu blocks for up to 1 hour to remove as much moisture as you can, changing the paper towels if necessary. Place the pressed blocks of tofu back in their containers, cover in plastic wrap, and freeze overnight. The next day, wrap the frozen tofu in a clean dishcloth or paper towels and defrost in the microwave for 10 minutes. Wrap in paper towels again and press for another 30 minutes.

Meanwhile, to make the marinade: In a large bowl, stir together the soy sauce, nutritional yeast, kelp granules, lemon juice, oil, and onion powder. Cut the tofu lengthwise into sticks, then toss in the marinade. Let sit in the marinade for 30 minutes to 1 hour.

While the tofu is marinating, make the breading: Fill one small bowl with the flour and cornstarch, another small bowl with the soy milk and vinegar, and a third small bowl with the panko, nutritional yeast, salt, onion powder, granulated garlic, paprika, and dried parsley.

CONT'D

Dredge the marinated tofu in the flour mixture, then the soy milk, back in the flour, back in the soy milk, and then *finally* in the panko mixture.

Line a plate with paper towels or set up a cooling rack. In a large skillet or sauté pan over medium-high heat, add the oil. Once heated to 350°F [180°C], fry the sticks in batches—about 1 minute per side—until brown and crispy. Place the fish sticks on the prepared plate or cooling rack.

Serve with vegan tartar sauce.

CHAPTER

2

Main Meals

Whether it's just another dinner with the family or a holiday gathering with all the trappings, sharing a meal is one of our most treasured human rituals. When I became a vegan in the '90s, this essential activity became difficult for our family. There weren't a ton of vegan options yet, and although our parents supported my dietary decision, it was no doubt a challenge for our mom to make food for the family and me at the same time. One of the big reasons Kale and I decided to open the Herbivorous Butcher was to offer meat analogs that were so good and so special that you would want to share them with your entire family. That way no one feels left out, and the home chef doesn't feel like an underpaid short-order cook. A lot of the meals you'll find in this chapter are the same ones we gobbled down as kids, but these are updated and cruelty-free!

—Aubry

Mujaddara Pot Roast

MAKES 3½ LB [1.6 KG]

Could anything bad happen when combining some of the most comforting foods from two different cultures? No, no, a million times no. It's like the Big Ole Beefy Beef (page 31) took a trip around the Middle East, came on home, put a tapestry up on its wall, covered itself in roasted cumin gravy, and started lying around on a bed of lentils, rice, and caramelized onions. Is it just a phase? Hope not.

Start with	
1 RECIPE	BIG OLE BEEFY BEEF [PAGE 31]
For the Mujaddara	
3 TBSP	VEGETABLE OIL
3 TBSP	BETTER BUTTER [PAGE 208]
2 LARGE	YELLOW ONIONS, THINLY SLICED
	SALT
1 CUP [200 G]	GREEN LENTILS, RINSED
4½ CUPS [1 L]	WATER
2 TBSP	CHICKEN BROTH POWDER [PAGE 200]
⅛ TSP	GROUND CINNAMON
PINCH OF	CARDAMOM
PINCH OF	ALLSPICE
1 CUP [200 G]	LONG-GRAIN RICE
	FRESH DILL, FOR GARNISH
	FRESH PARSLEY, FOR GARNISH
1 CUP [240 G]	PLAIN YOGURT, FOR GARNISH

HOW TO MAKE IT

Line a plate with paper towels.

Prepare the beef and bake as directed in the recipe.

While the beef bakes, make the Mujaddara: To a large pot over medium heat, add the oil and vegan butter. Once the butter is melted, add the onions and cook for about 15 minutes, stirring frequently and seasoning with salt. Once golden brown and caramelized, transfer half of the onions to the paper towel–lined plate to be used as garnish later.

Add the lentils, 3 cups [720 ml] of the water, and the chicken broth powder, the cinnamon, cardamom, and allspice to the remaining caramelized onions in the pot and stir to combine. Season with salt and bring to a boil, then lower the heat to a simmer, cover, and cook for 35 minutes, until the water is absorbed.

Once the lentils are done, add the rice to the pot along with the remaining 1½ cups [360 ml] of water and simmer for 15 minutes, until the rice is cooked.

CONT'D

Fluff before serving and season with more salt if desired. To serve, top the Mujaddara with the reserved caramelized onions, sliced beef, and some of the beef braising liquid and vegetables.

Garnish with fresh dill and parsley with the yogurt on the side, if desired. Store any extra in an airtight container and enjoy within a week.

Extra Credit

Here's your chance to add a twist to one of the flexy meat-made-without-meat bases. You can adapt the Mujaddara pot roast to a Lebanese palate by adapting these ingredients: ½ tsp ground cinnamon, 1 tsp ground allspice, ½ tsp ground cardamom, 1 tsp ground fennel, and 1 Tbsp orange zest.

Five-Spice Rib Tips

MAKES 1 LB [455 G]

Dust off that wok your aunt got you for your birthday ten years ago. Or pull out the skillet. Whatever. This Herbivorous Butcher shop favorite has graced many a rice bowl and is prepared to be the honored guest in yours. Your turn to cook it!

Start with	
1 LB [455 G]	THE RIB [PAGE 21]
For the Rib Tips	
6 TBSP [90 ML]	SUNFLOWER OIL
1	RED ONION, FINELY CHOPPED
8	GARLIC CLOVES, MINCED
1 CUP [240 ML]	MAPLE SYRUP
½ CUP [120 ML]	SOY SAUCE
3 TBSP	RICE VINEGAR
3 TBSP	FRESHLY SQUEEZED LIME JUICE
2 TBSP	CHINESE FIVE-SPICE POWDER
	SALT
	RICE, FOR SERVING
	CHOPPED FRESH CILANTRO, FOR GARNISH [OPTIONAL]

HOW TO MAKE IT

Prepare the ribs and cut them into bite-size pieces (or whatever size you'd like to eat) and set aside.

To make the rib tips: In a medium saucepan over medium-high, add 2 Tbsp of the oil. Once heated, add the onion and garlic; cook for a few minutes, until translucent. Add the maple syrup, soy sauce, vinegar, lime juice, Chinese five-spice, and another 2 Tbsp of oil; whisk well. Bring to a boil, then lower the heat to a simmer and cook for 5 minutes to allow the flavors to combine.

In a wok over medium-high, add the remaining 2 Tbsp of oil. Once heated, add the chopped ribs and stir-fry until the pieces begin to brown. Slowly add the sauce to the wok and stir-fry for a few more minutes, until the sauce has thickened and is coating the ribs. Season with salt.

Serve with rice and garnish with chopped cilantro, if desired. Store leftovers in an airtight container in the refrigerator and enjoy within 2 days.

Cherry-Glazed Rib Rack

MAKES 3 LB [1.4 KG]

Time to take that rib-making mastery for a sweet ride! The cherry barbecue glaze marries up with the savory ribs in a sublime union.

Start with	
1 RECIPE	THE RIB [PAGE 21]
For the Glaze	
2 TBSP	VEGETABLE OIL
1 MEDIUM	SWEET ONION, FINELY CHOPPED
5	GARLIC CLOVES, MINCED
PINCH OF	SALT
2½ CUPS [385 G]	FRESH OR FROZEN CHERRIES
1 CUP [240 ML]	KETCHUP
1 CUP [200 G]	BROWN SUGAR
¼ CUP [60 ML]	APPLE CIDER VINEGAR
1 TBSP	VEGAN WORCESTERSHIRE SAUCE
1 TSP	GROUND MUSTARD
½ TSP	FRESHLY GROUND BLACK PEPPER
SPLASH OF	LIQUID SMOKE
PINCH OF	DRIED BASIL
PINCH OF	GROUND CINNAMON
	ORANGE ZEST [OPTIONAL]

HOW TO MAKE IT

Prepare ribs and set aside. If you plan on baking the ribs, you can replace the braising broth in the Rib recipe with the cherry glaze and cook as directed.

To make the glaze: In a large saucepan over medium-high heat, add the oil. Once heated, add the onion, garlic, and salt and cook until fragrant, about 1 minute. Add the cherries, ketchup, brown sugar, vinegar, Worcestershire sauce, mustard, pepper, liquid smoke, basil, and cinnamon; whisk well to combine.

Simmer for 20 minutes, then process using an immersion or standard blender or food processor.

Add the orange zest (if using), then brush liberally onto your prepared rib recipe before grilling or baking. (Remember, the Rib is fully cooked already, so whatever additional cooking you do is only to impart flavor.)

If grilling, grill until lightly charred on both sides. If baking, preheat your oven to 375°F [190°C] and arrange your ribs in a single layer in the baking dish, then pour on the glaze (or chosen sauce), ensuring each one is almost completely covered. Cover the dish with foil and bake for 15 minutes. Turn and coat the ribs with glaze, and then bake for 10 minutes, uncovered. Remove from the pan, store in an airtight container, and enjoy within a week.

Lunch Plate Kahlua Pork

SERVES 6

The food cultures of Guam and Hawaii are kindred in spirit. One thing people of both islands definitely love is a good lunch plate— and Kahlua pork often takes center stage. And deservedly so. In our vegan version, jackfruit is a superstar stand-in for pork.

TWO 15 OZ [430 G] CANS	JACKFRUIT, DRAINED
¼ CUP [60 ML]	SOY SAUCE
¼ CUP [60 ML]	PINEAPPLE JUICE
2 TBSP	LIQUID SMOKE
	SALT
	FRESHLY GROUND BLACK PEPPER
3 TBSP	VEGETABLE OIL
	RED RICE, MACARONI SALAD, AND/OR GUAMANIAN SWEET BUNS, FOR SERVING [OPTIONAL]

HOW TO MAKE IT

Break apart large pieces of the jackfruit into a large bowl the best you can (you will have the opportunity to break it apart more once it's in the pan and heated). Add the soy sauce, pineapple juice, and liquid smoke; use your hands to combine thoroughly. Season with salt and pepper.

In a large pan over medium-low heat, add the oil. Once heated, toss in the jackfruit mixture. Turn up the heat to medium-high. Cook until the jackfruit is browned, 7 to 10 minutes. If you prefer smaller pieces of jackfruit, and for a more "pulled meat" style, break apart the jackfruit even further using a spatula.

Enjoy with red rice and macaroni salad or on a Guamanian sweet bun. Store in an airtight container in the refrigerator and enjoy within 1 week.

CONT'D

Jackfruit has recently exploded onto the vegan cooking scene, a welcome trend for those looking for a simple substitute for meat. That's because this funky, fibrous fruit has the consistency of shredded pork or chicken in its unripe stage. It also has a fairly neutral taste when young, so it takes up the flavor of whatever sauce or seasoning you pair it with. Don't look for this relative of the fig next to the oranges in the produce section, though. The chartreuse tropical fruit weighs in at a whopping 30 to 50 lb [13.5 to 22.5 kg]. Instead, look for it cut down to size in cans or refrigerated pouches at your local Asian market or health food store. Bonus: It's a decent source of protein and low in fat and calories.

Sizzlin' Malibu Chicken

SERVES 8 TO 10

Gotta pour one out for one of our favorite meals on Guam—Sizzler's Malibu Chicken. The restaurant chain ventured as far as Guam and from there into our hearts and veins. Who could blame any of us? This rich, breaded piece of heaven was often served with steak (as if) and a don't-stop-till-you-get-enough salad bar. This vegan version makes us so happy that we get cookin' by throwing on the song "Malibu" by Hole. Every. Time.

Start with	
1½ LB [680 G]	CHICKEN CUTLETS [PAGE 37]
For the Marinade	
2 CUPS [480 ML]	VEGAN BUTTERMILK [PAGE 207]
2	GARLIC CLOVES, MINCED
2 TSP	SALT
For the Breading	
⅓ CUP [75 G]	BETTER BUTTER [PAGE 208]
1 CUP [60 G]	PANKO BREAD CRUMBS
1 CUP [110 G]	GRATED VEGAN PARMESAN CHEESE
1 TBSP	DRIED PARSLEY
1 TBSP	GRANULATED GARLIC
2 TSP	SALT
2 TSP	FRESHLY GROUND BLACK PEPPER
8 TO 10 SLICES	SHAM [PAGE 51] OR VEGAN HAM
8 TO 10 SLICES	VEGAN SWISS OR SIMILAR CHEESE
For the Secret Mustard Sauce	
3 TBSP	VEGAN MAYONNAISE
2 TBSP	DIJON MUSTARD
1 TSP	YELLOW MUSTARD
2 TSP	SUGAR
	FRESH PARSLEY, FOR GARNISH [OPTIONAL]
	LEMON WEDGES, FOR GARNISH [OPTIONAL]

HOW TO MAKE IT

Prepare the cutlets and set aside.

To make the marinade: In a small bowl, mix the vegan buttermilk, garlic, and salt. Put the chicken in a 1 gal [3.8 L] resealable plastic bag or reusable equivalent. Pour in the buttermilk mixture; seal the bag and shake well to ensure even coating. Refrigerate for at least 4 hours or up to overnight.

Preheat your oven to 350°F [180°C].

To make the breading: Add the vegan butter to a 9 by 13 in [23 by 33 cm] baking dish and place in the oven to melt.

In a medium bowl, mix together the panko, Parmesan, parsley, granulated garlic, salt, and pepper.

With tongs, transfer the chicken from the bag to the breading bowl and coat well.

Bake, uncovered, in the buttered pan for 15 minutes on each side, until crispy. Once crispy, cover each piece of chicken with a slice of sham and Swiss cheese, then bake for 5 minutes more, until the cheese is melted.

CONT'D

While the chicken is baking, make the secret mustard sauce: In a small bowl, combine the vegan mayo, mustards, and sugar until incorporated.

Serve the chicken immediately out of the oven with the sauce and garnish with a bit of parsley and lemon wedges, if desired. Store any extra in an airtight container and enjoy within a week. **Tip:** An air fryer or 10 minutes in the oven at 350°F [180°C] will bring them right back to life.

Nana's Brown Paper Bag Fried Chicken

SERVES 2 TO 4

Summer days in Guam were usually spent with Nana, watching *The Price Is Right* while she was making all sorts of racket in the kitchen. There was one sound in particular that would always cause young Aubry's ears to perk up—and that was the sound of Nana shaking fried chicken in a paper bag. Sometimes the old ways are the best. So, shake a bag with us for Nana!

Start with	
1 LB [455 G]	CHICKEN CUTLETS [PAGE 37]
For the Marinade	
2 RECIPES	VEGAN BUTTERMILK [PAGE 207]
2	FLAX EGGS OR EQUIVALENT EGG SUBSTITUTE OF CHOICE [SEE PAGE 76]
For the Breading	
2 CUPS [280 G]	ALL-PURPOSE FLOUR
¼ CUP [30 G]	PAPRIKA
3 TBSP	WHITE PEPPER
2 TBSP	GARLIC POWDER
2 TBSP	POWDERED SUGAR
1½ TBSP	FRESHLY GROUND BLACK PEPPER
1½ TBSP	CELERY SALT
1 TBSP	GROUND GINGER
1 TBSP	GROUND MUSTARD
1 TBSP	SALT
2 TSP	DRIED THYME
2 TSP	DRIED BASIL
1 TSP	CAYENNE PEPPER
1 TSP	DRIED OREGANO
1 TSP	BAKING POWDER
	VEGETABLE OR SOYBEAN OIL, FOR FRYING

HOW TO MAKE IT

Prepare the cutlets and set aside.

To make the marinade: In a large bowl, mix together the vegan buttermilk and vegan eggs until well combined. Add the chicken, cover the bowl with plastic wrap or a lid, and refrigerate for at least 1 hour and up to 24 hours.

When you're ready to begin frying, make the breading: In a large bowl, combine the flour, paprika, white pepper, garlic powder, powdered sugar, black pepper, celery salt, ginger, mustard, salt, thyme, basil, cayenne, oregano, and baking powder.

Heat at least 3 in [7.5 cm] of oil in a heavy-bottom pan (we like to use a cast-iron skillet). Once heated to 350°F [180°C], turn the heat down to medium-low so the oil doesn't burn. Line a plate with paper towels.

CONT'D

One piece at a time, remove the chicken from the buttermilk, shake off excess liquid, and dredge in the breading. Then, dip the piece back into the buttermilk and again in the breading, then carefully drop into the oil. Fry each piece until golden brown and place it on the prepared plate. Repeat with the remaining chicken. Store remaining fried chicken in an airtight container in the refrigerator and enjoy within 1 week. Reheat chicken in an air fryer at 350°F [180°C] for 6 to 8 minutes or in the oven at 350°F [180°C] for 12 to 14 minutes until heated through.

FLAX EGG FACTS

For vegans, learning how to make a flax egg is a game changer. First, it's super easy: Just mix 1 Tbsp of flaxseed meal with 3 Tbsp of water and let it sit for 5 minutes. Boom! You now have the equivalent of one egg that's ready to use in so many recipes from muffins to smoothies to Nana's Brown Paper Bag Fried Chicken. Flaxseed meal is also loaded with omega-3 fatty acids, which promote heart and brain health. The flaxseed meal has a mild, nutty flavor, which enhances but doesn't overwhelm a recipe.

Mr. Cook Katsudon

SERVES 1

Katsudon (in Japanese: カツ丼) is a popular Japanese meal. It's a beautiful name for a bowl of rice topped with a deep-fried pork cutlet, egg, vegetables, and condiments. The dish takes its name from the Japanese words *tonkatsu* (pork cutlet) and *donburi* (rice bowl dish). Back on Guam, there was a tiny Japanese place with just nine seats at the bar, and it was fabulously called OK U Mr. Cook. The owner would always make a special bowl of katsudon for little Aubry without the bean sprouts. This is our rendition of the classic Japanese dish that would make little Aubry's heart soar—and still does.

Start with	
1	PATTY-SIZE CHICKEN CUTLET [PAGE 37] OR PORK CHOP [PAGE 35] OR TOFU
	VEGETABLE OIL, FOR FRYING
For the Tonkatsu	
½ CUP [70 G]	ALL-PURPOSE FLOUR
½ TSP	SALT
¾ CUP [180 ML]	JUST EGG PLANT-BASED EGG REPLACER
½ CUP [30 G]	PANKO BREAD CRUMBS
For the Donburi	
	VEGETABLE OIL, FOR FRYING
½ MEDIUM	YELLOW ONION, THINLY SLICED
½ CUP [120 ML]	DASHI BROTH [SEE PAGE 79]
3 TBSP	SOY SAUCE
2 TBSP	SAKE
1 TBSP	MIRIN
½ TBSP	SUGAR
ONE 12 OZ [360 ML] BOTTLE	JUST EGG PLANT-BASED EGG REPLACER
For the Assembly	
1½ CUPS [300 G]	COOKED SHORT-GRAIN WHITE RICE, WARM
	GREEN ONION, SLICED, FOR GARNISH
	TOGARASHI [JAPANESE SEASONING]

HOW TO MAKE IT

Prepare the chicken cutlet and set aside.

Set up a cooling rack or line a plate with paper towels. Add a ¼ in [6 mm] layer of oil to a heavy-bottom skillet and heat to 350°F [180°C].

To make the tonkatsu: In a shallow dish, mix together the flour and salt. Add the vegan egg to a second shallow dish and the panko to a third. Dredge the patty in the flour, then egg, then panko, making sure it's completely coated. Carefully drop it into the hot oil. Fry until golden brown. Drain on the cooling rack or prepared plate and set aside.

To make the donburi: In a small sauté pan or skillet over medium heat, add a small amount of oil. Once heated, add the onion and sauté until translucent. Add the dashi, soy sauce, sake, mirin, and sugar and bring to a boil. Lower the heat to medium-low. Slice the tonkatsu patty and add it to the pan. Pour in the vegan egg and let cook until it sets in the middle and around the edges, 3 to 4 minutes. (It will look a little runny, but it's just the sauce that gives it that appearance.)

CONT'D

To assemble: Put the warm cooked rice into a ramen-style bowl and slide the egg and tonkatsu mixture onto the top, allowing the sauce to pour in with it. Garnish with green onions and togarashi.

Pro Tip

This meal serves one; just double everything for two people. You will need two small skillets or sauté pans as well. You can also make the sauce mixture in one separate pot, then split it into two pans if that makes it easier.

DASHI BROTH

This recipe uses dashi broth, which is super easy to make and can be used in lots of recipes. To make it, you'll need a package of dried kombu seaweed, available online or at any Asian market. Boil the kombu in water for 30 minutes. Strain the kombu from the broth and discard in the compost. The broth will smell fishy (because, duh, it's seaweed), so don't fret. You can store leftover broth for up to 1 week to make tempura sauce, miso soup, or more ramen.

Easy Cheezy Supreme Pizza Bowls

MAKES 1 PIZZA BOWL

Have you ever secretly, selfishly wanted a decadent deep-dish pizza all for yourself? How about if it required no cooking skills whatsoever? Pizza bowls are a great way to get what you want with only a fraction of the usual pizzamaking effort. They are built upside down, starting with the toppings, and you can use whatever you like, making the possibilities endless. I'm a fan of this one—a good ole supreme pizza, hold the mushrooms. —*Aubry*

Start with	
1 OZ [30 G]	PEPPERONI [PAGE 41]
For the Pizza Bowl	
	OLIVE OIL, FOR BRUSHING
2 OZ [55 G]	VEGAN MOZZARELLA OR PROVOLONE CHEESE, SHREDDED
1 OZ [30 G]	VEGAN ITALIAN SAUSAGE, CRUMBLED OR CHOPPED
2 TBSP	CHOPPED GREEN BELL PEPPER
1 TBSP	CHOPPED RED ONION
1 TBSP	SLICED BLACK OLIVES
½ CUP [120 ML]	PIZZA SAUCE
1 RECIPE	KALE'S PIZZA DOUGH [PAGE 204] OR VEGAN READY-MADE DOUGH

HOW TO MAKE IT

Preheat the oven according to the baking temperature of the pizza dough you've chosen.

Prepare the pepperoni and set aside.

To make the pizza bowl: Brush a 10 oz [285 g], ovenproof bowl with olive oil, making sure to grease the entire bowl inside and out. Into the bowl, add the vegan cheese, vegan sausage, pepperoni, bell pepper, onion, and black olives. Next spoon on the sauce, making sure to cover all the ingredients.

Stretch the pizza dough over the top of bowl, draping it over the sides so that the top and outside are completely covered. Brush the pizza dough with olive oil. Place the bowl on a baking sheet and bake according to the directions of the dough you've chosen.

Once the dough is golden and crisp, remove from the oven and flip your pizza bowl face-down onto a plate. Carefully remove the bowl—it will be hot—and gaze at the perfect deep-dish pizza you just created.

CHAPTER 3

Sides

If you're anything like Kale and me, side dishes are every bit as important as the main event. In fact, for a vegan, these supporting players can often be the superstars of the meal. How many times have you, our fellow plant eaters, gone to a restaurant and taken a peek at the menu only to hungrily page to the side-dish options because none of the mains were animal-free? Bless that side of asparagus! (Hold the butter.) And bring on that baked potato! (Hold the butter and the sour cream, please.) Over the years we've become true connoisseurs of those lifesaving sides. We've determined the dishes that we love best and figured out how to make them every bit as buttery and creamy as the ones found on any menu! In this case, bring on the extra vegan butter and sour cream, please!

—Aubry

Garlic Egg Fried Rice

SERVES 2 TO 4

Nothing could be simpler than cooking up some rice with vegan egg, garlic, onions, and a splash of soy sauce, but if you want to do it justice, you better use the right pan and hit the right temps at the right times. Don't screw this up, because you and this dish have so much potential.

3 TBSP	PEANUT OIL OR VEGETABLE OIL
8	GARLIC CLOVES, MINCED
4 CUPS [800 G]	DAY-OLD COOKED RICE
1 CUP [240 ML]	JUST EGG PLANT-BASED EGG REPLACER
¼ TSP	SALT
	FRESHLY GROUND BLACK PEPPER
	WHITE PEPPER
1	GREEN ONION, WHITE AND GREEN PARTS, THINLY SLICED

HOW TO MAKE IT

In a wok over medium-low heat, add the oil. Once heated, add the garlic and cook until crispy and fragrant, 2 to 4 minutes. Remove the garlic from the pan and set aside.

Add the rice to the pan and fry, stirring to coat the rice with the garlic oil. Cook until the rice is heated through, 5 to 7 minutes.

Push the rice to the sides of the pan, creating an opening in the middle. Pour the vegan egg into the opening and let cook until it begins to set. Using a wooden spoon or spatula, move the egg around until fully cooked, then chop apart using the spatula and stir the eggs and rice together.

Add the salt and fried garlic, season with black and white pepper, and stir until combined.

Garnish with green onions and serve on the side or as your main dish! Leftovers? Store in an airtight container in the refrigerator and serve within 3 days.

CONT'D

Pro Tip

Enjoy as a side or add a vegan protein, such as tofu or vegan chicken, and some peas and carrots to make this super side into a super meal. For a kick, we also like to add chile oil or fresh Thai chiles before serving.

THE WONDERS OF THE WOK

Ahhhh, the wok. And to think that for most of my life I would fry rice or make pad Thai in a skillet. In retrospect, if I could've chosen to either learn how to walk or learn "how to wok" at a young age, I would've chosen the latter. A quality, well-cared-for wok will last a lifetime—and will reward you for all the love you put into it with an indescribable depth of flavor. Just be sure to stay away from the nonstick woks (the food won't taste right). Before yours makes its maiden voyage, be sure to season it well in a very well-ventilated space!

—Kale

Red Rice

SERVES 8 TO 10

There wasn't a day that went by that there wasn't a pot of rice sitting on Nana's stove. We ate rice for every meal, including breakfast (don't knock it until you try it!). But on Sundays we got the best rice—red rice. Red and earthy thanks to the achiote seeds, this Chamorro recipe has never missed a fiesta in the history of its life. It's both the foundation and the life of the party.

3 TBSP	ACHIOTE SEEDS
2½ CUPS [600 ML]	ROOM-TEMPERATURE WATER
2 CUPS [400 G]	UNCOOKED SHORT-GRAIN WHITE RICE
2 TBSP	SUNFLOWER OIL
½ CUP [115 G]	ROUGHLY CHOPPED VEGAN BACON
½	YELLOW ONION, DICED
3 TBSP	SALT

HOW TO MAKE IT

Soak the achiote seeds overnight in the water.

When ready to cook the rice, first rinse the rice a few times in cold water in your rice cooker pot or a 4 qt [3.8 L] lidded pot; this will help make the rice less starchy. Drain the water and set the pot of rice aside.

In a sauté pan or skillet over medium-high heat, add the oil and cook the vegan bacon for 3 to 5 minutes, or until fragrant. Remove the bacon and set aside, leaving the oil in the pan.

Add the onion to the oil and cook for 2 minutes, or until translucent.

Add the cooked onion and remaining oil from the pan to the rice cooker or pot with the uncooked rice; stir until the rice is coated. Add the salt and stir until combined.

With a mesh strainer, strain the seeds from the achiote water and discard the seeds. Pour the water into the pot.

CONT'D

Press the start button on your rice cooker and cook until the button pops, or bring the rice pot to a boil on the stove, then turn the heat to low and cover. Simmer for 20 minutes or until the water has been absorbed completely.

When the rice is finished cooking, add the bacon to the rice and serve. Store leftovers in an airtight container in the refrigerator and enjoy within 3 days.

THE RISE OF THE RICE COOKER

The invention of the rice cooker is an epic tale that reads like a movie trailer: "In a world where Japanese women labor for hours every morning to make rice for the day, one woman fights to find a better way." In short, if there is an easier way to make something *and* it turns out perfect every time, then do it that way. If you've never succumbed to this small appliance's charm, you owe it to yourself to make room in the cupboard.

DIY ACHIOTE WATER

You'll bump into achiote (a.k.a. annatto) in a lot of Mexican and Caribbean dishes. It's a pretty little spice and a natural coloring agent (hello, yellow!) that's extracted from the seeds of an evergreen shrub. Sold in seed, powder, or paste form, it has a mildly sweet and earthy flavor. It's often infused in oil to bring its color and flavor to stews and rice dishes. This recipe calls for achiote water, which you can make by adding 1 tsp of seeds to ¼ cup [60 ml] of boiling water. Just remove the water from the heat once it boils and let the seeds steep for 30 minutes before straining them out.

Cheezy Garlicky Truffly Smashed Potatoes

SERVES 2 TO 4

We'd like this delicious and tummy-filling ditty to be an ode to the "sides" section of every restaurant menu: May we forever be in your debt for the lifesaving vegan options you gave us throughout the 1990s and early 2000s.

1½ LB [680 G]	SMALL POTATOES, SKIN ON
	SALT
½ CUP [110 G]	VEGAN BUTTER
4	GARLIC CLOVES, CHOPPED
1 TBSP	CHOPPED FRESH PARSLEY, PLUS MORE FOR SERVING
	FRESHLY GROUND BLACK PEPPER
½ CUP [50 G]	VEGAN PARMESAN CHEESE
	TRUFFLE OIL, AS MUCH AS YOU DAMN WELL PLEASE

HOW TO MAKE IT

Scrub up your potatoes. Place them in a large pot of salted water and bring to a boil. Cook, covered, for 20 to 25 minutes, or until tender. Drain well.

Preheat the oven to medium-high broil. If you do not have a broil function, preheat your oven to 450°F [230°C]. Grease a baking sheet.

Melt the vegan butter in a microwave or on the stove, if you prefer. Add the garlic and parsley.

Arrange the potatoes on the prepared baking sheet and, using a fork or potato masher, lightly smash each potato. Make sure the potatoes remain in one piece.

CONT'D

Spoon the butter mixture over each potato, then season with salt and pepper and top with vegan Parmesan.

Broil the potatoes in the oven until they are crispy and golden, 12 to 15 minutes. Remove from the oven and drizzle truffle oil all over them.

Serve with a sprinkling of parsley and salt. Store leftovers in an airtight container in the refrigerator and enjoy within 5 days.

Smoked Cheezy Grits

SERVES 2 TO 4

Maybe you're like the two-years-ago us and think grits are a bland, diner side dish plopped on plates mostly down South. We learned far too late that grits are for real the tastiest corn dish in all the world—if you treat them right. Let's add a little smoky vegan Cheddar and give them the respect they deserve.

2¼ CUPS [540 ML]	VEGAN CHICKEN BROTH OR VEGETABLE BROTH
1½ CUPS [360 ML]	UNSWEETENED NONDAIRY CREAMER OR UNSWEETENED COCONUT MILK
1 TSP	WHITE PEPPER
¼ TSP	CHILI POWDER
¾ CUP [105 G]	QUICK GRITS
4 TBSP [55 G]	VEGAN BUTTER
½ CUP [40 G]	SHREDDED VEGAN CHEDDAR OR VEGAN CHEESE OF CHOICE
1	JALAPEÑO, SEEDED AND DICED
2 TSP	NUTRITIONAL YEAST FLAKES
¼ TSP	FRESHLY GROUND BLACK PEPPER
⅛ TSP	LIQUID SMOKE
	GREEN ONIONS, BOTH WHITE AND GREEN PARTS, CHOPPED, FOR GARNISH
	SMOKED PAPRIKA, FOR GARNISH

HOW TO MAKE IT

In a large pot over medium heat, combine the broth, nondairy creamer, white pepper, and chili powder; bring to a boil.

Once boiling, stir in the grits, vegan butter, vegan cheese, jalapeño, nutritional yeast, black pepper, and liquid smoke. Lower the heat to medium-low and simmer for 2 to 3 minutes, until the grits have thickened.

Add more broth or grits depending on how thick you like your grits.

Top with green onions and a pinch of smoked paprika and serve immediately.

Bacon Creamed Corn

SERVES 6 TO 8

Bacon, cream, corn. Are there any other ingredient combos quite as dreamy as this? This recipe makes a great side for fried chicken or any barbecue plate you can imagine. We all know corn is more starch than vegetable, but I think for the sake of a complete meal let's call it a vegetable this one time.

3 TBSP	VEGETABLE OIL
5 SLICES	VEGAN BACON, CHOPPED
3 TBSP	VEGAN BUTTER
3	GARLIC CLOVES, MINCED
2	SHALLOTS, MINCED
¼ CUP [35 G]	ALL-PURPOSE FLOUR
2¼ CUPS [540 ML]	UNSWEETENED NONDAIRY MILK
1 TBSP	BROWN SUGAR
	SALT
	FRESHLY GROUND BLACK PEPPER
TWO 1 LB [455 G] BAGS	FROZEN CORN, THAWED, OR 2 LB [910 G] FRESH CORN KERNELS
1 CUP [80 G]	SHREDDED VEGAN CHEESE
1 TBSP	CHOPPED FRESH CHIVES

HOW TO MAKE IT

In a large skillet over medium-low heat, add the oil. Once heated, add the vegan bacon and cook until crispy, making sure it doesn't burn. Remove the bacon and set aside, reserving 1 Tbsp of bacon oil.

In a medium pot over medium-low heat, melt the vegan butter and add the reserved bacon oil. Add the garlic and shallots; cook for 2 to 3 minutes, or until fragrant. Add the flour and cook until lightly browned, whisking constantly for about 1 minute. Slowly whisk in the nondairy milk and continue whisking until the mixture begins to thicken, 3 to 4 minutes. Stir in the sugar and season the mixture with salt and pepper. Stir in the corn, lower the heat, and simmer until thickened completely, 8 to 10 minutes, stirring often.

Ladle into bowls and garnish with vegan cheese, chives, and the reserved bacon. Store leftovers in an airtight container in the refrigerator and enjoy within 1 week.

A Lotta Elote

SERVES 4 TO 6

Like so many of the most delicious recipes, this grilled corn-on-the-cob treat is inspired by the caravan of food trucks in East L.A. It's simply the perfect fresh and fast summer food. We spent more time trying to come up with a decent pun for the name of this recipe than we spent developing it—and the recipe took a couple of weeks.

¼ CUP [60 ML]	SOY SAUCE
2 TBSP	VEGETABLE OIL
10 TO 12	WHOLE SHISHITO PEPPERS
4 TO 6	EARS OF CORN, HUSKED
⅓ CUP [75 G]	THAT YUMMI YUMMI SAUCE THOUGH . . . [PAGE 214] OR VEGAN MAYONNAISE
¼ CUP [60 G]	VEGAN SOUR CREAM
1 TSP	ANCHO CHILE POWDER, PLUS MORE FOR GARNISH
½ CUP [50 G]	GRATED VEGAN PARMESAN CHEESE
⅓ CUP	CHOPPED FRESH CILANTRO, PLUS MORE FOR GARNISH
2	GARLIC CLOVES, MINCED
	SALT
	LIME WEDGES, FOR GARNISH

HOW TO MAKE IT

In a medium bowl, mix the soy sauce and oil; toss in the shishito peppers and set aside.

Heat a gas or charcoal grill to medium and place a pan on the grill top. Grill the corn for about 6 minutes, turning frequently to ensure all sides are charred. Set aside to cool.

Throw the marinated shishito peppers onto the grill pan and grill for 6 to 8 minutes, turning occasionally until they're blistered and charred. Set aside to cool.

In a large bowl, combine the Yummi Yummi sauce, vegan sour cream, ancho chile powder, vegan Parmesan, cilantro, and garlic and stir well to combine.

Once the shishitos and corn are cool, cut the kernels off the cobs and coarsely chop the shishitos. Transfer to the large bowl with the Yummi Yummi mixture, toss well to combine, and season with salt.

Garnish with a bit of cilantro, a pinch of ancho chile powder, and the lime wedges. Serve immediately.

Chamorro Macaroni Salad

SERVES 6 TO 8

In most cases, we feel there's some play, some inventiveness and individuality, involved in creating a dish. Not so much with macaroni salad. In our world, it must be a certain way. It can't be too sweet or mustardy, too soggy or too dry. The noodle shape is important—and how much mayo you add and when you add it can change everything. There's an art to it. Bottom line: Follow these directions closely, or else.

1 TBSP	SALT, PLUS MORE FOR THE PASTA WATER
ONE 1 LB [455 G] BOX	SMALL ELBOW MACARONI
2 CUPS [480 G]	VEGAN MAYONNAISE
¼ CUP [65 G]	SWEET RELISH
2 TBSP	CHOPPED PIMENTOS
½ TBSP	FRESHLY GROUND BLACK PEPPER
¾ TSP	YELLOW MUSTARD
⅛ TSP	ONION POWDER
⅛ TSP	GARLIC POWDER
⅛ TSP	BROWN SUGAR
8 OZ [225 G]	EXTRA-FIRM TOFU, DICED

HOW TO MAKE IT

Bring a large pot of generously salted water to a boil and cook the macaroni to al dente according to the instructions on the box. Drain and set aside to cool.

Once the macaroni is at room temperature, add the vegan mayo, relish, pimentos, black pepper, salt, mustard, onion powder, garlic powder, and brown sugar; mix until well combined.

Add the diced tofu and carefully combine; try not to crumble the tofu too much as you mix.

Chill in the refrigerator and serve cold. Store in an airtight container in the refrigerator for up to 5 days.

Pro Tip

In a hurry to get to the picnic? Soak noodles in cold water for a few minutes before boiling to speed up the cooking process.

Gollai Hagun Suni

SERVES 6

Confession: We can't even say the name of this dish. But, dear god, you have to trust us—you've never had spinach this decadent and full of flavor. Coconut and turmeric bring the lowly spinach leaf to the heights of its full potential.

1 TBSP	VEGETABLE OIL
1	YELLOW ONION, THINLY SLICED
2 CUPS [40 G]	FRESH BABY SPINACH
1	JALAPEÑO PEPPER, SLICED CROSSWISE
¼ TSP	MINCED PEELED FRESH GINGER
TWO 15 OZ [430 G] CANS	COCONUT MILK
2 TBSP	GROUND TURMERIC
2 TBSP	FRESHLY SQUEEZED LEMON JUICE
1 TSP	SALT
½ TSP	CAYENNE PEPPER
2 TBSP	HOT PEPPER PASTE [OPTIONAL]
1 TSP	TOASTED SESAME OIL [OPTIONAL]
1 TSP	CHILE OIL [OPTIONAL]

HOW TO MAKE IT

In a sauté pan over low heat, add the oil. Once heated, add the onion and cook until translucent, 2 to 3 minutes.

Add the spinach, jalapeño, and ginger; turn down the heat to low and cover. Cook until the spinach is just wilted, 3 to 4 minutes. Shake up the cans of coconut milk before opening. Add the coconut milk to the spinach mixture and stir until combined. Add the turmeric, lemon juice, salt, and cayenne and stir. Turn up the heat to medium-low and cook until heated through, 3 to 5 minutes. If you like spice, stir in the hot pepper paste, sesame oil, and chile oil. (For a milder version, just stick with the jalapeño.)

Store leftovers in an airtight container in the refrigerator and enjoy within 3 days.

Pro Tip

Turn this into a complete meal by adding tofu or your favorite meat alternative, such as vegan chicken.

CHAPTER 4

Soups

Big pots of boiling goodness have been a part of life since humans figured out how to make fire. Soups are comforting and warm; they make us feel better when we're sick or having a bad day. Ah heck, they make us feel better even if we're in tip-top shape and having an amazing day! We've heard it said that soup is good for the soul. We tend to agree. These recipes have healed us since we were little people, and we hope they'll do the same for you (and your little people). Here's the difference—they are rich, satisfying, and soul soothing using only vegan broths and ingredients.

Make a Dal with the Devil

SERVES 4

The truth is, I went down to the crossroads and sold my soul to the devil for his dal recipe. For years, I've been making dal for myself but couldn't figure out why it didn't taste like it did at the Indian restaurants. I just had to know. Then it hit me like a bolt from above: Adding the tempering (*tadka*, or spices cooked in oil for maximum flavor) at the end makes all the difference. The optional dhungar method to smoke the finished dal adds a depth deeper than the Pit itself (but for heaven's sake, do it in a well-ventilated area). —*Kale*

For the Devilish Dal Stew	
1 CUP [200 G]	SPLIT PIGEON PEA LENTILS [*TUVAR DAL*]
3 CUPS [720 ML]	WATER
1 MEDIUM	ONION, DICED
2 MEDIUM	TOMATOES, DICED
2	ANAHEIM PEPPERS, SEEDED, DERIBBED, AND VERY THINLY SLICED
2	GARLIC CLOVES, MINCED
2 TBSP	CHICKEN BROTH POWDER [PAGE 200]
1 TSP	MINCED PEELED FRESH GINGER
½ TSP	GROUND TURMERIC
½ TSP	GARAM MASALA
¼ TSP	HING POWDER [ASAFOETIDA]
¼ CUP [10 G]	FRESH CILANTRO, CHOPPED, PLUS MORE FOR GARNISH
2 TBSP	UNSWEETENED VEGAN HALF-AND-HALF
For the Optional Dhungar Method [a.k.a. Smoke in the Cauldron]	
1 PIECE	NATURAL CHARCOAL
½ TSP	VEGETABLE OIL

For the Tadka [Spice Topping] to Temper the Devil	
¼ CUP [60 ML]	VEGETABLE OIL
2 TSP	WHOLE CUMIN SEEDS
6	GARLIC CLOVES, MINCED
¼ CUP [28 G]	RED PEPPER FLAKES
1 TSP	CAYENNE
¼ TSP	HING POWDER [ASAFOETIDA]
For the Assembly	
	BASMATI RICE, FOR SERVING

HOW TO MAKE IT

To make the devilish dal stew: Rinse the lentils and put them into a pressure cooker or Instant Pot. Add the water, onion, tomatoes, peppers, garlic, broth powder, ginger, turmeric, garam masala, and hing powder. Stir to combine.

Pressure-cook for 30 minutes, or until the lentils become soft and creamy.

CONT'D

Sitr and mash the vegetables and lentils with a whisk or slotted spoon, then cook for 2 to 3 minutes more, until the desired consistency is reached.

Add the cilantro and vegan half-and-half, stirring to combine.

To make the optional dhungar method: Put the small piece of charcoal over an open flame until red-hot. With a pair of tongs, carefully place the charcoal in a small ramekin or bowl and float it on top of your dal in the pressure cooker. Pour the vegetable oil on top of the charcoal and quickly cover your pressure cooker for 1 to 2 minutes so that the contents are fully smoked. Carefully remove the ramekin from the pressure cooker before dishing out the dal.

To make the (much-recommended!) spice topping: In a skillet or sauté pan over medium-high heat, add the vegetable oil. Once heated, add the cumin seeds and cook until crackling and fragrant. Add the garlic, red pepper flakes, cayenne, and hing powder. Turn down the heat to low.

To assemble: Add the spice topping to the dal, garnish with the remaining cilantro and, if you're still conscious after this process, serve with basmati rice and enjoy. Leftovers keep in the refrigerator in an airtight container for up to 1 week.

CONT'D

Make a Dal with the Devil is a crazy-good concoction that owes its crazy-goodness to these staples of Indian cuisine.

Dal—Dal is both an ingredient and a dish. It refers to a type of dry split pea or lentil and a yummy, spiced stew made from simmering them until they are broken down.

Tuvar dal (toover dal or toor dal)—Known as a pigeon pea, tuvar dal is a skinned and split pea. It's the most widely used form of lentil, thanks to its thick, gelatinous, almost meaty consistency.

Garam masala—This Indian spice blend translates loosely to "warming spices." It's a ground mix of coriander seeds, cumin, black peppercorns, mace (similar to nutmeg), cardamom, bay leaves, and cinnamon sticks.

Hing powder (asafoetida)—This dark brown gummy substance comes from the root of the ferula plant, an herb related to celery and parsley. It's processed into a coarse yellow powder that smells like boiled eggs, but don't let that stop you. Once cooked, it turbocharges other flavors in your dish with a powerful punch of umami.

Chinese Ramen with Sweet & Sour Fried Tofu

SERVES 2 TO 4

Winter in Minnesota is no joke, but we keep ourselves warm with this made-from-scratch ramen. Its perfectly blended spice profile will leave everyone so speechless, you can all eat happily without interruption.

For the Broth	
12	DRIED WHOLE CHILES
8	WHOLE CLOVES
4	BAY LEAVES
3	STAR ANISE PODS
1	CINNAMON STICK
1 TBSP	SICHUAN PEPPERCORNS
2 TBSP	VEGETABLE OIL
2	GARLIC CLOVES, HALVED
2 TBSP	CHILE GARLIC SAUCE OR PASTE [MORE IF YOU LIKE IT HOTTER]
6 SLICES	PEELED FRESH GINGER, OR ½ TBSP PREPARED MINCED GINGER
8 CUPS [2 L]	VEGAN BEEF BROTH OR VEGETABLE BROTH
For the Sweet & Sour Fried Tofu	
	OIL, FOR FRYING
1 BLOCK [455 G]	EXTRA-FIRM TOFU
1 CUP [140 G]	ALL-PURPOSE FLOUR
2 CUPS [480 ML]	SWEET-AND-SOUR SAUCE
2 CUPS [120 G]	PANKO BREAD CRUMBS
1 TSP	RED PEPPER FLAKES
For the Ramen	
10 OZ [285 G]	FRESH OR DRY RAMEN NOODLES
	BABY BOK CHOY LEAVES OR SPINACH [ENOUGH FOR EACH BOWL]
	FRIED GARLIC CHIPS [SEE PRO TIP], FOR GARNISH
	SLICED GREEN ONIONS, FOR GARNISH
	CHILE OIL, FOR GARNISH [OPTIONAL]
	CRUSHED PEANUTS, FOR GARNISH [OPTIONAL]

HOW TO MAKE IT

To make the broth: Combine the chiles, cloves, bay leaves, star anise pods, cinnamon stick, and peppercorns in a spice sachet.

In a large heavy-bottom pot over medium-low heat, add the oil. Once heated, add the garlic, chile garlic sauce, and ginger. Cook until fragrant, 2 to 3 minutes, stirring often to prevent burning. Pour in the broth and bring to a boil. Once boiling, throw in the spice sachet. Cover the pot, turn down the heat, and simmer the broth for 30 minutes.

While the broth simmers, make the fried tofu: In a cast-iron or heavy-bottom skillet, add about 2 in [5 cm] of oil and heat until it registers 350°F [180°C] on a probe thermometer (see Pro Tip). Set up a cooling rack near the stove or line a plate with paper towels.

CONT'D

Drain the tofu and wrap it in paper towels to absorb excess water. Put the flour, sweet-and-sour sauce, and panko each in their own separate shallow dish for dredging. Add the red pepper to the panko.

Cut the tofu into 1½ in [4 cm] cubes. Dredge one cube at a time on all sides, first in the flour, then the sweet-and-sour sauce, and finally the panko. Once all the tofu cubes are dredged, carefully drop them into the hot oil a few at a time. Fry until golden brown, 2 to 3 minutes. Use a spider or a slotted spoon to remove the tofu from the oil, and place on the cooling rack or prepared plate. Reserve the oil to fry the garlic chips (see Pro Tip).

To make the ramen: When your broth is fragrant, remove and discard the spice sachet. Cook the ramen noodles according to the package instructions.

To prepare each bowl (and you'll want big bowls for this), place the ramen noodles and whatever leafy vegetable you chose in the bottom.

Ladle in broth over the noodles and vegetables. Add in as much tofu as you'd like on top.

Garnish with the garlic chips and green onions. We like to garnish with a bit of chile oil and crushed peanuts as well.

If you have leftover broth, you can put it into a mason jar or other glass container and refrigerate it for up to 3 days.

Pro Tip

We like to use a probe thermometer to make sure the oil temperature is at 350°F [180°C], but the trick of carefully dropping a water droplet in the oil to see if it sizzles will work too. To make fried garlic chips, slice 2 or 3 garlic cloves and fry in 350°F [180°C] oil until golden brown and crisp, 1 to 2 minutes. Transfer to a paper towel–lined plate with a slotted spoon to drain.

Spicy Tantanmen Ramen

SERVES 2

Inspired by numerous viewings of the classic Japanese film *Tampopo*, Aubry had to try her hand at the ramen game. This is the first step on a road of a thousand bowls of ramen, but it is a road worth walking, we promise! —*Kale*

For the Spicy Crumbled Pork	
1 CUP [95 G]	TEXTURED VEGETABLE PROTEIN [TVP]
¾ CUP [180 ML]	DASHI BROTH [SEE PAGE 79]
2 TBSP	SOY SAUCE
1 TSP	SESAME OIL
1 TSP	CHILE OIL
1 TSP	VEGETABLE OIL
1	GARLIC CLOVE, CHOPPED
1 TSP	PEELED FRESH MINCED GINGER
For the Ramen	
2 CUPS [480 ML]	VEGETABLE STOCK
1 CUP [240 ML]	DASHI BROTH [SEE PAGE 79]
2 TSP	SAKE
1½ TSP	WHITE MISO PASTE
½ TSP	MIRIN
10 OZ [285 G]	RAMEN NOODLES
3 TBSP	ASIAN SESAME PASTE
3 TBSP	SOY SAUCE
1 TBSP	CHILE OIL
2 TSP	RICE VINEGAR
	SLICED GREEN ONIONS, FOR TOPPING [OPTIONAL]
	CRUSHED PEANUTS, FOR TOPPING [OPTIONAL]
	FRIED GARLIC CHIPS, FOR TOPPING [OPTIONAL; SEE PRO TIP, PAGE 114]
	SESAME OIL, FOR TOPPING [OPTIONAL]
	CHILE OIL, FOR TOPPING [OPTIONAL]

HOW TO MAKE IT

To make the spicy crumbled pork: In a medium bowl, rehydrate the TVP with the dashi broth, soy sauce, sesame oil, and chile oil. Combine until the TVP is moist.

In a sauté pan or skillet over medium-low heat, add the vegetable oil, garlic, and ginger and cook until fragrant, 3 to 4 minutes. Add the TVP mixture and stir to combine. Fry until browned and crisp, about 8 minutes, stirring to make sure all sides are browning. Set aside.

To make the ramen: In a large pot over medium-low heat, combine the stock, dashi broth, sake, miso, and mirin. Cook until heated through, 5 to 7 minutes.

Meanwhile, prepare your ramen noodles using the directions on the package. Now is the time to fry garlic chips, if using. (We'd highly recommend it—see the Pro Tip on page 114.)

In a medium bowl, whisk together the sesame paste, soy sauce, chile oil, and vinegar and divide the mixture between two ramen bowls. Ladle the desired amount of broth into each bowl, add the noodles to each bowl, and top with the TVP mixture and any other toppings you like. Go crazy!

CONT'D

Make room in your pantry for kombu. One of the many sea vege-tables (read: seaweed) harvested in the cold waters surround-ing Japan, kombu is a versatile type of kelp that can be used to give recipes a rich umami boost. Kombu broth—or dashi—is as quintessential in Japan as mom's chicken broth. Sold in strips like its cousin nori (which holds together sushi), kombu is a nutritional powerhouse that comes packed with vitamins and minerals such as vitamin A, vitamin C, iron, and calcium. It's the glutamic acid that makes the sea goody mildly salty and subtly sweet, which enhances other flavors and tenderizes proteins—heck, it even takes the gas out of beans. The magical vegetable will also wait patiently in your pantry for months when stored in an airtight container.

Textured vegetable protein is the super-sexy name of a product that blew the minds of vegans and vegetarians alike in the 1960s. This high-fiber, high-protein meat substitute is made from soy flour. When it's rehydrated and cooked, it takes on the texture of ground meat. And because it absorbs spices and flavors well, you can doll it up in any way you see fit. Look for it in the bulk foods section of natural food stores and co-ops, or the baking aisle of your grocery store.

Lake Minne-Tom-Ka

SERVES 4 TO 6

We take the quintessential Thai comfort food, tom ka, and make it a little more substantial for those of us in the frozen northlands of the United States. This marriage of cultures is a beautiful thing. Our East-meets-North version is richer than Bezos and more warming than a heated blanket on a cold winter night.

2 TBSP	BETTER BUTTER [PAGE 208]
3 MEDIUM	CARROTS, DICED
1 MEDIUM	YELLOW ONION, DICED
3	GARLIC CLOVES, MINCED
1	RED POTATO, DICED
¼ CUP [50 G]	CHICKEN BROTH POWDER [PAGE 200]
TWO 13½ OZ [385 G] CANS	COCONUT MILK
8	KAFFIR LIME LEAVES
ONE 6 TO 8 IN [15 TO 20 CM]	LEMONGRASS STALK, FINELY CHOPPED
1 PIECE [25 G]	PEELED FRESH GALANGAL [THAI GINGER], SLICED
¼ CUP [60 ML]	UNSWEETENED VEGAN HALF-AND-HALF
½ CUP [120 ML]	WATER
1 BLOCK [400 G]	SOFT TOFU, DICED
1 CUP [90 G]	BROCCOLI FLORETS
½ CUP [60 G]	GREEN PEAS [FRESH OR FROZEN]
½ CUP [30 G]	DICED MUSHROOMS
1 SMALL	ZUCCHINI, DICED
1 SMALL	YELLOW SQUASH, DICED
1 TSP	BLACK PEPPER
	SALT
	JASMINE RICE, FOR SERVING

HOW TO MAKE IT

In a large stockpot over medium heat, add the vegan butter. Once melted, add the carrots, onion, garlic, and potato. Cook, stirring, until the onions start to get translucent, 2 to 3 minutes. Add the broth powder, stirring to combine. Add the coconut milk slowly, stirring while you pour to combine.

Place the kaffir lime leaves, lemongrass, and galangal in a spice sachet. Add the spice sachet to the pot.

Add the vegan half-and-half, water, tofu, broccoli, peas, mushrooms, zucchini, yellow squash, and black pepper and stir to combine. Bring the pot to a boil, then lower the heat to a simmer. Simmer over low heat for 35 minutes, until the zucchini and squash are fork-tender.

Take out your spice sachet (unless you really want to eat some cheesecloth).

Season with salt and serve atop jasmine rice. Leftovers can be stored in an airtight container in the refrigerator for up to 1 week.

Wintery White Chicken Chili

SERVES 6 TO 8

Growing up on Guam, I didn't have much exposure to chili. When I moved to Minnesota, I learned how much everyone loved it! For years I've been trying to make a chili that I could also love. I found the answer: this oh-so-unconventional white chili! It's creamy. It's warm. It's perfect. —*Aubry*

Start with	
1 LB [455 G]	CHICKEN CUTLETS [PAGE 37] OR STORE-BOUGHT CHICKEN SUBSTITUTE
For the Chili	
2 TBSP	OLIVE OIL
1	YELLOW ONION, CHOPPED
2	GARLIC CLOVES, MINCED
1¾ TSP	GROUND CUMIN
1 TSP	GROUND CORIANDER
1 TSP	KOSHER SALT
½ TSP	BLACK PEPPER
½ TSP	WHITE PEPPER
4 CUPS [1 L]	VEGAN CHICKEN BROTH OR VEGETABLE BROTH
TWO 15 OZ [430 G] CANS	GREAT NORTHERN BEANS
2 CUPS [280 G]	FRESH OR FROZEN CORN
ONE 4 OZ [115 G] CAN	GREEN CHILES, DRAINED
1½ CUPS [360 G]	NONDAIRY SOUR CREAM
1 CUP [80 G]	SHREDDED VEGAN CHEESE, FOR GARNISH
1	JALAPEÑO PEPPER, CHOPPED, FOR GARNISH [OPTIONAL]
	GREEN ONIONS, FOR GARNISH
	FRESH CILANTRO, FOR GARNISH

HOW TO MAKE IT

Chop or shred the vegan chicken cutlets and set aside.

To make the chili: In a large pot over medium-low heat, add the olive oil. Once heated, add the onion and garlic and cook until fragrant, 2 to 3 minutes. Add the chicken. Cook until lightly browned. Add the cumin, coriander, salt, black pepper, and white pepper. Stir until combined. Stir in the broth, beans, corn, and chiles and bring to a simmer.

Simmer for 10 to 15 minutes, until thickened. Remove the pot from the heat and stir in the nondairy sour cream.

Serve the chili in bowls. Divide the vegan cheese and jalapeño slices, if desired for extra heat, evenly among the bowls. Garnish with green onions and cilantro.

Store leftovers in an airtight container in the refrigerator and enjoy within 5 days.

Pro Tip

We like to serve this dish with rice, but fresh tortillas chips are also great alongside it.

Coconut Chicken Chilakelis Soup

SERVES 6

The corn may be American-grown, but this recipe comes from our home island of Guam, which is a melting pot of cultures. This mini melting pot is filled with savory broth, toasted ground rice, and shredded chicken. No matter how hot it gets on Guam, there is always a time for a warm and comforting soup.

Start with	
1 LB [455 G]	CHICKEN CUTLETS [PAGE 37]
For the Soup	
2 CUPS [400 G]	SHORT-GRAIN WHITE RICE
1 TBSP	VEGETABLE OIL
1 LARGE	ONION, DICED
5	GARLIC CLOVES, FINELY CHOPPED
4 CUPS [960 ML]	ACHIOTE WATER [SEE PAGE 90]
7 CUPS [1.7 L]	VEGAN CHICKEN BROTH
8	THAI CHILES, CHOPPED [OR MORE OR LESS DEPENDING ON DESIRED HEAT LEVEL]
2½ TBSP	WHITE VINEGAR
1 TSP	BLACK PEPPER
½ TSP	WHITE PEPPER
½ TSP	SALT
ONE 14 OZ [400 G] CAN	COCONUT MILK
	CHOPPED GREEN ONION, FOR GARNISH [OPTIONAL]
	STORE-BOUGHT FRENCH-FRIED ONIONS, FOR GARNISH [OPTIONAL]
	CHILE OIL, FOR GARNISH [OPTIONAL]

HOW TO MAKE IT

Once the vegan chicken is prepared, chop or shred the cutlets and set them aside.

To make the soup: In a large pan over medium-high heat, toast the rice until golden brown and fragrant. Let the rice cool, then grind it in a food processor or blender.

In a heavy-bottom stockpot over medium heat, add the oil. Once heated, add the onion and garlic. Sauté for 5 minutes, or until translucent. Add the chicken and cook until slightly browned, 5 to 7 minutes.

Slowly add the achiote water and bring to a boil. Add the broth and ground rice. Simmer for 10 minutes. **Note:** The soup will thicken once the rice is added.

Add the Thai chiles, vinegar, black pepper, white pepper, salt, and coconut milk. Stir to combine and simmer until heated through, 5 to 7 minutes.

Divide the soup among bowls. Top each bowl with green onions, French-fried onions, or chile oil, if desired, and serve immediately. Store any leftovers in an airtight container in the refrigerator and enjoy within 5 days.

Ope! Minnesota Creamy Turkey Wild Rice Soup

SERVES 6 TO 8

Minnesota is known for its wild rice soup. Surprised? You won't be when you learn that wild rice was harvested as a staple food by the Indigenous people of this area for centuries. In 1977, it finally got its due by being named the state's official grain. History lesson complete. The important thing to remember is that this soup is a winter warmer for the record books. We're nominating it as the Official Vegan Wild Rice Soup of Minnesota. Once you try it, you'll second that—or at least have seconds of this.

⅓ CUP [80 ML]	OLIVE OIL
1	YELLOW ONION, CHOPPED
2 TBSP	MINCED GARLIC
1 CUP [140 G]	ALL-PURPOSE FLOUR
6 CUPS [1.4 L]	VEGAN CHICKEN BROTH OR VEGETABLE BROTH
4 CUPS [720 G]	COOKED WILD RICE
2 CUPS [220 G]	CHOPPED OR CUBED VEGAN TURKEY OR HAM
1½ CUPS [170 G]	SHREDDED CARROTS
½ CUP [70 G]	BLANCHED AND SLICED RAW ALMONDS
¼ TSP	RED PEPPER FLAKES
2 CUPS [480 ML]	UNSWEETENED NONDAIRY CREAMER OR UNSWEETENED COCONUT MILK
	SALT
	FRESHLY GROUND BLACK PEPPER

HOW TO MAKE IT

In a large, heavy-bottom pot over medium heat, add the olive oil. Once heated, stir in the onion and garlic and cook until the onion is translucent, about 5 minutes. Add in the flour slowly, whisking constantly. Cook for 3 minutes more. Slowly whisk in the broth until no clumps remain and the consistency is smooth, then bring to a boil. Turn down the heat to medium-low and simmer for 10 minutes, stirring frequently.

Add the rice, vegan turkey, carrots, almonds, and red pepper flakes. Return the soup to a simmer and cook until the carrots are tender, about 5 minutes.

Stir in the nondairy creamer or coconut milk and cook until warmed through, 5 to 7 minutes. Season with salt and pepper before serving. Store leftovers in an airtight container in the refrigerator and enjoy within 1 week.

"Juicy Lucy" Cheeseburger Chili

SERVES 4

Sometimes you just need it, you know? That ultra-cheesy, extra-meaty bowl of warmth is simply a must-have. You can't be sad with a bowl of this goodness, a nice blanket, and some *X-Files* reruns, eh? It's worked for us, and we want to believe it will work for you too.

Start with	
1 LB [455 G]	GROUND BEEF [PAGE 33]
For the Chili	
3 TBSP	VEGETABLE OIL
1	GREEN BELL PEPPER, DICED
1 LARGE	SWEET ONION, DICED
5	GARLIC CLOVES, MINCED
	SALT
	FRESHLY GROUND BLACK PEPPER
3 TBSP	CHILI POWDER
1 TSP	SMOKED PAPRIKA
½ TSP	GROUND CUMIN
¼ CUP [65 G]	KETCHUP
¼ CUP [65 G]	DILL PICKLE RELISH
2 TBSP	YELLOW MUSTARD
2 TBSP	BUTCHER-STRENGTH WORCESTERSHIRE [PAGE 228]
2 CUPS [320 G]	PINTO BEANS, DRAINED
ONE 14½ OZ [415 G] CAN	CRUSHED TOMATOES
¾ CUP [180 ML]	WATER
¾ CUP [180 ML]	CHEESE SAUCE BASE [PAGE 203]
3 TBSP	BEEF BROTH CONCENTRATE [PAGE 199]
	STORE-BOUGHT FRENCH-FRIED ONIONS, FOR TOPPING
	SHREDDED VEGAN CHEESE, FOR TOPPING

HOW TO MAKE IT

Prepare the vegan ground beef and set it aside.

To make the chili: In a large pot over medium heat, add the oil. Once heated, toss in the bell pepper, onion, and garlic. Sprinkle with just a pinch of salt and pepper. Once the onion begins to get translucent, 2 to 3 minutes, add the ground beef. Stir well to combine. Add the chili powder, paprika, and cumin and cook for a few more minutes until the ground beef begins to brown. Add the ketchup, relish, mustard, and Worcestershire and stir well. Add the beans, tomatoes, water, cheese sauce base, and broth concentrate. Stir well to combine.

Bring to a boil, then lower the heat to a simmer. Cook for 30 minutes over medium-low heat with the lid slightly ajar.

Serve hot with French-fried onions and shredded vegan cheese on top. Store any leftover chili in an airtight container in the refrigerator and enjoy within 1 week.

Nana's Beef Stew

SERVES 6 TO 8

Every year on our grandma's birthday, we make her stew. It's our loving and delicious tribute to her, filled with all the things that she loved—especially the three different starches: potatoes, pasta, and rice.

Start with	
12 OZ [340 G]	PORTERHOUSE STEAK [PAGE 27] OR OTHER VEGAN BEEF
For the Stew	
1 TBSP	OLIVE OIL
1 MEDIUM	YELLOW ONION, CHOPPED
2 CUPS [280 G]	PEELED AND CHOPPED CARROTS
1	GARLIC CLOVE, MINCED
¼ TSP	SALT, PLUS MORE FOR SEASONING
ONE 28 OZ [800 G] CAN	WHOLE PEELED TOMATOES
8 CUPS [2 L]	BEEF BROTH CONCENTRATE [PAGE 199] OR VEGETABLE BROTH
2	RUSSET POTATOES, PEELED AND CUT INTO LARGE CHUNKS
1½ CUPS [225 G]	SMALL MACARONI NOODLES
	FRESHLY GROUND BLACK PEPPER
	SHORT-GRAIN WHITE RICE, FOR SERVING [OPTIONAL]

HOW TO MAKE IT

Cut the vegan steak into chunks and set aside.

To make the stew: In a large pot or Dutch oven over medium-low heat, add the oil. Once heated, add the onion, carrots, and garlic. Cook for 3 to 5 minutes or until fragrant. Sprinkle in the salt. Add the steak and cook for about 3 minutes, or until the beef is browned. Stir in the tomatoes and broth; bring to a boil. Once boiling, stir in the potato chunks and macaroni noodles. Bring to a boil again and cook until the potatoes and macaroni are tender, 6 to 8 minutes.

Season with salt and pepper and serve with rice, if desired, or as is. Store leftovers in an airtight container in the refrigerator and enjoy within 3 days.

CHAPTER
5

For a Crowd

Back in 2020 BC (Before Covid), we gathered without a thought, not to mention a mask. Now, throwing together a casserole to feed—and impress—a large group of favorite people seems like the ultimate reward for those long, lonely days we endured. So, if the coast is clear, let's potluck! Let's picnic! Let's party! Even better, we truly hope you're digging into this cookbook at a coffee shop, planning your next get-together, surrounded by wonderful strangers' faces. To celebrate, here are a plethora of recipes for you to *share* with old faces and new faces and the faces you love.

—Aubry

Kale's Very Fine Lasagna

SERVES 4 TO 6

Ah, the old Ace in the Hole. The vegan Trojan Horse. The Very Fine Lasagna. When I had one last shot to convince my girlfriend's parents that I wasn't a total loser, I brought over this pantheon of Italian comfort and went from zero to hero with one cheesy, meaty lasagna pan of power. This saucy ninja will sneak past the defenses of any die-hard meat-eater, leaving them begging for seconds. —*Kale*

Start with	
ONE 12 OZ [340 G] BOX	LASAGNA NOODLES
	SALT
For the Red Sauce	
3 TBSP	OLIVE OIL
2	RED ONIONS, FINELY CHOPPED
6	GARLIC CLOVES, MINCED
	SALT
10	ROMA TOMATOES, DICED, OR ONE 28 OZ [800 G] CAN CRUSHED TOMATOES
TWO 6½ OZ [185 G] CANS	TOMATO SAUCE
TWO 6 OZ [170 G] CANS	TOMATO PASTE
1 LB [455 G]	GROUND SEITAN
1 BUNCH	FRESH BASIL, STEMMED AND CHOPPED, PLUS MORE FOR GARNISH
1 BUNCH	FRESH ITALIAN PARSLEY, CHOPPED, PLUS MORE FOR GARNISH
2 TBSP	CANE SUGAR
1 TBSP	FENNEL SEEDS
2 TSP	ITALIAN SEASONING
½ TSP	BLACK PEPPER
For the Assembly	
1	VEGAN EGG EQUIVALENT
8 OZ [230 G]	VEGAN RICOTTA CHEESE
8 OZ [230 G]	VEGAN MOZZARELLA CHEESE OR SIMILAR, SLICED
8 OZ [230 G]	VEGAN MOZZARELLA CHEESE, SHREDDED
1 CUP [240 ML]	CHEESE SAUCE BASE [PAGE 203]
¼ CUP [25 G]	GRATED VEGAN PARMESAN CHEESE [OPTIONAL]

HOW TO MAKE IT
Preheat the oven to 350°F [180°C].

Place the lasagna noodles into a 9 by 13 in [23 by 33 cm] baking dish, cover with warm water and a bit of salt, and let sit for 20 minutes until malleable. Drain and set the noodles aside.

Meanwhile, to make the red sauce: In a large pot over medium-high heat, add the oil. Once heated, add the onion, garlic, and a pinch of salt and cook for 2 to 3 minutes, or until the onion is translucent.

Add the tomatoes, tomato sauce, and tomato paste, stirring well to combine. Add the seitan, basil, parsley, sugar, fennel, Italian seasoning, and black pepper. Stir well, then season with salt.

Let the sauce simmer for a few minutes (or as long as you have time for; the longer the better, up to 2 hours).

CONT'D

To assemble: Grease the same 9 by 13 in [23 by 33 cm] baking dish with olive oil or nonstick spray.

In a medium bowl, mix the vegan egg with the vegan ricotta, whisking well to combine.

On the bottom of the greased baking pan, evenly spread about 3 cups [720 g] of the prepared red sauce. Layer six lasagna noodles lengthwise over the red sauce, overlapping slightly. Evenly spread the ricotta mixture over the lasagna noodles. Layer half of the sliced vegan mozzarella over the ricotta. Ladle another 3 cups [720 g] of red sauce on top of the mozzarella. Repeat the layers once more.

Top with the shredded mozzarella, cheese sauce, and vegan Parmesan. Cover the pan with foil.

Bake for 30 minutes, then remove the foil and bake for an additional 20 minutes.

Garnish with minced basil and parsley and serve. Store leftovers in an airtight container in the refrigerator and enjoy within 1 week.

Pro Tip

If possible, let the assembled, unbaked lasagna sit in the refrigerator overnight to allow the flavors to combine.

Picture yourself in a tiny galley-style commercial kitchen. It's hot as hell, three alarms are going off, you've already worked a double today, and the person on the opposite side of the kitchen just started launching food out of an open blender. Just then, "Halo" comes on shuffle and suddenly the clouds part and anything seems possible. Welcome to the infancy of the Herbivorous Butcher and allow us to introduce you to a playlist of songs that got us through the hard times and provide the perfect soundtrack for your party!

This playlist can be found on Spotify: **Cooking with the Vegan Butchers**.

"Get Ready"—Rare Earth
"Life on Mars?"—David Bowie
"Just the Two of Us" (ft. Bill Withers)
　—Grover Washington
"Never Tear Us Apart"—INXS
"Everytime You Go Away"—Paul Young
"Rock and Roll All Nite"—KISS
"Halo"—Beyoncé
"Rose Garden"—Lynn Anderson
"This is America"—Childish Gambino
"I Try"—Macy Gray
"Head Over Heels"—Tears for Fears
"I Would Die 4 U"—Prince
"Started from the Bottom"—Drake
"Hornets! Hornets!"—The Hold Steady
"Private Eyes"—Hall & Oates
"Only You"—Yaz
"Sugar, We're Goin' Down"—Fall Out Boy
"Always Something There to Remind Me"
　—Naked Eyes
"Human"—The Human League
"Heroes"—David Bowie
"Jump in the Line"—Harry Belafonte
"Formation"—Beyoncé
"I Miss You"—blink-182
"Mamma Mia"—ABBA
"Dance Yrself Clean"—LCD Soundsystem
"All Black Everything"—Lupe Fiasco
"Do Ya"—Electric Light Orchestra
"Your Little Hoodrat Friend"—The Hold Steady
"Insensitive"—Jann Arden
"If I Could Turn Back Time"—Cher
"Changes"—2Pac, Talent
"Good as Hell"—Lizzo
"Freedom!"—George Michael
"'Till I Get There"—Lupe Fiasco
"Fight the Power"—Public Enemy

"Dancing in the Street"—Martha Reeves
　and the Vandellas
"Dancing in the Moonlight"—King Harvest
"Live It Out"—Metric
"Kokomo"—The Beach Boys
"Dancing on My Own"—Robyn
"Rainbowarriors"—CocoRosie
"Dreams"—The Cranberries
"Plea from a Cat Named Virtue"
　—The Weakerthans
"Maniac (Instrumental)"—Peaches, Moullinex
"Parallel or Together"—Ted Leo and
　the Pharmacists
"Songbird"—Kenny G
"Let Me Back In"—Rilo Kiley
"Barcelona"—Freddie Mercury, Mike Moran,
　Monsterrat Caballé
"Our Retired Explorer"—The Weakerthans
"City Grrrl"—CSS, ft. Ssion
"Paper Planes"—MIA
"Wrecking Ball"—Miley Cyrus
"Left and Leaving"—The Weakerthans
"If It Makes You Happy"—Sheryl Crow
"Polyester Bride"—Liz Phair
"Anthems for a Seventeen-Year-Old Girl"
　—Broken Social Scene
"Bring Me to Life"—Evanescence
"Mercy"—Kanye West, ft. Big Sean, 2 Chainz,
　Pusha T
"Werewolf"—CocoRosie
"Look What You Made Me Do"—Taylor Swift
"The Sweet Escape"—Gwen Stefani, Akon
"Boss"—Rick Ross, Dre
"Labor of Love"—Ned Doheny
"Till the World Ends"—Britney Spears
"Nothing's Gonna Stop Us Now"—Starship
"Eat It"—"Weird Al" Yankovic

Pinky-Up Smashed Potato Hot Dish

SERVES 4 TO 6

You can't call yourself a Mighty Midwesterner without a family hot dish recipe. Whatever would you bring to potlucks?! Let's just say, this kind of fancy crowd-pleaser has national—if not inter-national—appeal and can hold its own in both a stuffy church basement and a stuffy dinner party.

Start with	
14 OZ [400 G]	PORTERHOUSE STEAK [PAGE 27] OR OTHER VEGAN BEEF SUBSTITUTE
For the Hot Dish	
1 RECIPE	CHEEZY GARLICKY TRUFFLY SMASHED POTATOES [PAGE 91], OR 1 LB [455 G] BAG OF TATER TOTS
3 TBSP [45 G]	VEGAN BUTTER
1	SHALLOT, CHOPPED
3	GARLIC CLOVES, CHOPPED
1 TSP	DRIED THYME
½ CUP [120 ML]	RED WINE, SUCH AS MERLOT OR CABERNET
1 CUP [130 G]	FRESH ENGLISH PEAS
1 CUP [125 G]	DIAGONALLY SLICED CARROTS
5 OZ [140 G]	VEGAN BACON, CHOPPED
For the Béchamel Sauce	
3 TBSP	VEGAN BUTTER
3 TBSP	ALL-PURPOSE FLOUR
2 CUPS [480 ML]	UNSWEETENED NONDAIRY MILK
	SALT
	FRESHLY GROUND BLACK PEPPER
1 TBSP	WHITE TRUFFLE OIL, PLUS MORE FOR DRIZZLING
	DRIED PARSLEY, FOR GARNISH

HOW TO MAKE IT

Chop the vegan steak and set it aside.

For the hot dish: We like to top this hot dish with the smashed potatoes recipe instead of tater tots, so get those going while you prep this. It times out perfectly if you get the potatoes boiling, then start prepping the rest. Tater tots prepared to package directions also work, so get those cooking now too.

In a cast-iron skillet over medium-low heat, add the vegan butter. Once melted, add the shallot and garlic and cook until translucent and fragrant, 3 to 4 minutes. Turn up the heat to medium-high, add the steak and thyme, and cook for 3 to 5 minutes, until the steak begins to brown. Turn down the heat to medium and slowly pour in the wine, using a wooden spoon to scrape up the bits stuck to the pan. Cook until the wine is mostly evaporated. Stir in the peas, carrots, and half of the vegan bacon. Cook for another 3 to 5 minutes until heated through. Turn off the heat.

Your potatoes should be done boiling, so get those smashed, topped, and under the broiler now!

CONT'D

Preheat the oven to 350°F [180°C].

Next, you'll quickly make your béchamel sauce: In a medium saucepan over medium-low heat, melt the butter. Once melted, slowly add in the flour while continuously whisking, until completely combined and the mixture is lightly browned. Then slowly whisk in the nondairy milk until combined. Turn down the heat to low and cook until the sauce is thickened, about 10 minutes. Season with salt and pepper—you'll need more salt than you think. Finally, add in the truffle oil and whisk to combine.

To assemble: Pour the béchamel sauce over the steak and vegetable mixture in the skillet and top with the crispy smashed potatoes and remaining vegan bacon.

Bake for 25 minutes. Garnish with parsley and serve.

Store leftovers in an airtight container in the refrigerator and enjoy within 5 days.

Ritzy Chicken Casserole

SERVES 6

Growing up in the 1980s and '90s, it seemed like everyone was always trying to add popular snacks to their food: cornflake-crusted this and potato chip–topped that. Here's your chance to do it by putting on the Ritz—and with a fancy truffle twist to boot!

Start with	
3 CUPS [400 G]	ROUGHLY CHOPPED CHICKEN CUTLETS [PAGE 37]
For the Casserole	
3 TBSP	VEGAN BUTTER
24	RITZ CRACKERS, CRUMBLED
⅓ CUP [80 ML]	OLIVE OIL, PLUS MORE FOR SAUTÉING
1 LB [455 G]	ASPARAGUS, CHOPPED
1 MEDIUM	ONION, CHOPPED
2	GARLIC CLOVES, CHOPPED
¾ CUP [105 G]	ALL-PURPOSE FLOUR
2½ CUPS [600 ML]	VEGETABLE BROTH
¾ CUP [180 ML]	UNSWEETENED NONDAIRY MILK
¾ CUP [180 ML]	LIGHT, DRY WHITE WINE, SUCH AS SAUVIGNON BLANC
1 CUP [240 G]	NONDAIRY SOUR CREAM
	TRUFFLE OIL

HOW TO MAKE IT

Preheat the oven to 375°F [190°C]. Grease a 9 by 13 in [23 by 33 cm] baking dish.

To make the casserole: In a sauté pan or skillet over medium-low heat, add the vegan butter. Once melted, add in the crumbled crackers. Stir until the cracker crumbs are completely coated in the butter. Set aside.

Wipe out the pan, return to medium-low heat, and add 2 Tbsp of the olive oil. Once heated, add the chopped vegan chicken cutlets and asparagus. Cook for 3 to 5 minutes, until the chicken is browned a bit. Spoon the mixture into the prepared baking dish. Set aside.

In a medium saucepan over medium heat, add the ⅓ cup [80 ml] olive oil. Once heated, add the onion and garlic; cook for 3 to 5 minutes or until translucent. Slowly add the flour, whisking constantly until combined. The roux may be a bit lumpy. Cook for a couple of minutes until the flour is toasted. Slowly pour in the broth while whisking until completely combined. Bring to a boil and cook for a few minutes until the mixture is thickened and coats the back of a spoon. Slowly add in the nondairy milk while whisking until completely combined. Do the same with the wine. Cook until heated through. Finally, stir in the nondairy sour cream.

CONT'D

Pour the mixture over the chicken and asparagus. Top with buttery Ritz mixture and bake for 30 minutes. Remove from the oven and drizzle with the truffle oil.

Serve family style! Leftovers can be stored in an airtight container in the refrigerator for 5 days.

TRUFFLE LOVE

Not everyone loves truffles, but those who do (ahem, Aubry) love them enough to fork over a stack of hard-earned dollars to enjoy them. What's to love and why the high price tag? The flavor (and aroma!) of truffle is like nothing else: earthy, umami bombed, with a kind of nuttiness and a hint of garlic. Add it to the right recipe, and you've just elevated even the humblest dish to haute cuisine.

The stiff cost is a result of how tough it is to find the unsightly fungus; it cleverly hides underground on tree roots. Truffle oil, while still expensive, is a more affordable way to enjoy its unique taste (and aroma!). Fun(gi) fact: Truffle, the chocolate version, is so named because of its resemblance to the real deal.

The Mighty Chicken Enchilada Casserole

SERVES 4 TO 6

I have a love-hate relationship with enchiladas. Here's the deal: I can't eat them fast enough, so the corn tortillas just end up becoming one with the sauce before I'm halfway through 'em! One day I decided I was going to win. Those enchiladas were not going to take me down! I turned those suckers into a casserole; if it will all become one, let it begin as one. Enchilada, meet Casserole! —*Aubry*

Start with	
1½ CUPS [200 G]	DICED OR SHREDDED CHICKEN CUTLETS [PAGE 37] OR JACKFRUIT
For the Crust	
¾ CUP [105 G]	YELLOW CORNMEAL
1 CUP [240 ML]	COLD WATER
2 CUPS [480 ML]	VEGAN CHICKEN BROTH OR VEGETABLE BROTH
2 TBSP	VEGAN BUTTER
½ TSP	SALT
For the Filling	
1 TBSP	OLIVE OIL
1	YELLOW ONION, DICED
2	GARLIC CLOVES, CHOPPED
1	POBLANO OR GREEN PEPPER, DICED
ONE 15 OZ [430 G] CAN	WHITE BEANS, RINSED AND DRAINED
1 CUP [140 G]	FROZEN OR CANNED WHOLE-KERNEL CORN
½ CUP [90 G]	SLICED GREEN OLIVES
ONE 15 OZ [340 G] JAR	GREEN ENCHILADA SAUCE
½ CUP [120 ML]	UNSWEETENED NONDAIRY MILK
1½ CUPS [120 G]	SHREDDED VEGAN CHEDDAR CHEESE, PLUS MORE AS NEEDED

HOW TO MAKE IT

Preheat the oven to 350°F [180°C]. Grease a 9 by 13 in [23 by 33 cm] baking dish.

To make the crust: In a medium bowl, combine the cornmeal and cold water. Whisk until mixed thoroughly.

In a medium saucepan, bring the broth to a boil. Stir in the cornmeal mixture and turn down the heat to low. Add the vegan butter and salt. Cover and cook the mixture over very low heat for 35 minutes, stirring occasionally.

Spoon the mixture into the prepared baking dish. It should fill the bottom third of the dish. Set aside.

To make the filling: In a sauté pan or skillet over medium-low heat, add the olive oil. Once heated, add the onion and garlic and cook for 3 to 5 minutes, until fragrant, stirring as needed. Add the diced vegan chicken and poblano pepper. Cook until the chicken begins to brown a bit, 3 to 5 minutes, then stir in the beans, corn, and green olives.

CONT'D

Once combined, add the enchilada sauce and heat through for 2 to 3 minutes. While stirring, slowly add in the nondairy milk. Cook until heated through, then stir in 1 cup [80 g] of the vegan cheese until melted and combined thoroughly.

Pour the mixture into the prepared baking dish and fill to just below the rim to avoid spillover during baking. Top with the remaining ½ cup [40 g] of cheese, adding more if you'd like.

Cover with foil and bake for 50 minutes. Then remove the foil and bake for an additional 10 minutes.

Serve family style, topped with a little extra shredded cheese!

Store in an airtight container in the refrigerator and enjoy within 5 days.

GOT (THE RIGHT) MILK?

When you're making savory foods that call for an unsweetened nondairy milk, be sure to purchase one that is truly unsweetened. We like to use unsweetened soy milk that contains just two simple ingredients: soybeans and water. There are unsweetened versions of most nondairy milks, but keep an eye on the grams of sugar listed in the nutrition facts, or you'll be using lots of salt to counteract that sweetness.

Hobbits of the Shire Shepherd's Pie

SERVES 6 TO 8

"Boil 'em, mash 'em, stick 'em in a stew!" Or better yet, stick those po-ta-toes on top of a decadent shepherd's pie that would be worthy of serving to Sam and Frodo upon their glorious return to the Shire.

Start with	
1 LB [455 G]	GROUND BEEF [PAGE 33] OR STORE-BOUGHT VEGAN GROUND BEEF
For the Mashed Potato Topping	
3	RUSSET POTATOES, PEELED AND CUBED
	SALT
4 TBSP [60 G]	VEGAN BUTTER
¼ CUP [60 ML]	UNSWEETENED NONDAIRY MILK
¼ CUP [20 G]	VEGAN SHREDDED CHEESE
¼ TSP	GARLIC POWDER
	FRESHLY GROUND BLACK PEPPER
For the Filling	
2 TBSP	OLIVE OIL
1 MEDIUM	YELLOW ONION, CHOPPED
2	GARLIC CLOVES, MINCED
3 TSP	DRIED PARSLEY
1½ TSP	DRIED THYME
1 TSP	DRIED ROSEMARY
2½ TBSP	TOMATO PASTE
2 TBSP	BUTCHER-STRENGTH WORCESTERSHIRE [PAGE 228]
1 TSP	SMOKED PAPRIKA
2 TBSP	ALL-PURPOSE FLOUR
1½ CUPS [200 G]	FROZEN PEAS AND CARROTS
½ CUP [70 G]	FROZEN CORN
1 CUP [240 ML]	VEGAN BEEF BROTH OR VEGETABLE BROTH
½ CUP [120 ML]	LAGER BEER
	FRESHLY GROUND BLACK PEPPER

HOW TO MAKE IT

Preheat the oven to 350°F [180°C].

Prepare the vegan ground beef and set aside.

To make the mashed potato topping:
Place the potatoes in a medium saucepan and add cold water to cover by at least 1 in [2.5 cm]. Add ½ tsp of salt to the water. Turn up the heat to high and bring the water to a boil. Turn down the heat to low to maintain a simmer and cover. Cook for 15 to 20 minutes, or until you can easily poke through the potatoes with a fork.

While the potatoes are cooking, in a medium sauté pan or skillet over medium heat, heat the vegan butter and the non-dairy milk until the butter is melted. (You can also heat them in a microwave.) Watch that the mixture does not boil.

When the potatoes are done, drain the water and place the steaming-hot potatoes in a large bowl. Pour the melted butter mixture over the potatoes. Using a potato masher or a fork, mash the potatoes until there are no lumps. Stir in the vegan cheese and garlic powder and season with salt and pepper. Set aside.

CONT'D

To make the filling (which comes together quickly): In a large sauté pan or skillet over low to medium heat, add the olive oil. Once heated, add the onion, garlic, parsley, thyme, and rosemary. Cook for 3 minutes, or until fragrant. Add the ground beef, tomato paste, Worcestershire, and paprika. Combine well and cook for 3 to 5 minutes, or until the ground beef begins to brown. Sprinkle the flour over the meat mixture and stir until combined. Stir in the frozen veggies, then pour in the broth and beer; stir to combine and bring to a simmer. Cover and turn down the heat to low; cook for an additional 5 minutes. The mixture should thicken a bit. Season with black pepper to taste.

Spoon the mixture into a pie dish or an 8 by 8 in [20 by 20 cm] baking dish, leaving space on top for the mashed potatoes. Spoon the mashed potatoes on top, smoothing with the back of the spoon. Save any leftover meat mixture and mashed potatoes for later—or make a second small pie for a friend!

Store leftovers in an airtight container in the refrigerator and enjoy within 5 days.

BLT Couscous Crust Quiche

SERVES 4 TO 6

On a warm spring Sunday, there's nothing better than a light and lovely quiche. But we find that the crust can really weigh you down and might get in the way of that after-brunch badminton game—or just send you straight to nap town. Your salvation comes in the form of this quiche, with its deliciously deceiving couscous crust. (Just kidding, this quiche is delicious no matter what season, day of the week, meal—and with or without badminton involved.)

2 TBSP	VEGAN BUTTER, MELTED
2 CUPS [330 G]	COOKED COUSCOUS
	SALT
	FRESHLY GROUND BLACK PEPPER
2 TBSP	OLIVE OIL
4 SLICES	VEGAN BACON, CHOPPED
4	GARLIC CLOVES, CHOPPED
ONE 12 OZ [360 ML] BOTTLE	JUST EGG PLANT-BASED EGG REPLACER
¾ CUP [180 ML]	UNSWEETENED NONDAIRY MILK
1 TSP	DIJON MUSTARD
½ CUP [50 G]	SHREDDED VEGAN PARMESAN CHEESE
⅛ TSP	KALA NAMAK (BLACK SALT)
2 CUPS [40 G]	FRESH BABY SPINACH
1	ROMA TOMATO, SLICED

HOW TO MAKE IT

Preheat the oven to 375°F [190°C].

Pour the melted vegan butter over the cooked couscous and season with salt and pepper.

Press the couscous mixture into a pie pan to form a crust.

In a sauté pan or skillet over medium-low heat, add the olive oil. Once heated, sauté the vegan bacon and garlic for 3 to 4 minutes, or until fragrant. Sprinkle evenly over the pressed crust.

In a medium bowl, combine the vegan egg, nondairy milk, mustard, ¼ cup [25 g] of the vegan Parmesan, and the kala namak. Season with pepper and whisk until combined.

Put the spinach into the pie crust and pour the egg mixture over the spinach. Arrange the sliced tomatoes on the uncooked pie and sprinkle with remaining ¼ cup [25 g] of Parmesan.

CONT'D

Bake for 45 minutes to 1 hour or until the egg has set.

Store leftovers in an airtight container in the refrigerator and enjoy within 5 days.

WHAT IS KALA NAMAK?

Kala namak (a.k.a. black salt or Himalayan black salt) hails from the salt mines of the Himalayas. It doesn't come by its blackish color naturally, however. That comes from firing pink Himalayan salt (considered one of the purest salts on the planet) with a mix of activated charcoal, herbs, and spices. Used in Ayurvedic medicine, kala namak has antioxidant properties that aid liver function and digestion. This rock salt is also surprisingly low in sodium—good news for those with high blood pressure. Due to its sulfur content, kala namak lends recipes a mild, egg-like flavor. Today the salt is also made synthetically, so read the label before you buy.

Fondue You Wanna Dip

MAKES 5 CUPS [1.2 L]

We missed a lot during the age of social distancing. For some of us, fondue was a big one. Who doesn't love huddling together without a care in the world, dipping little skewers of vegan meat, veggies, and bread into one burning-hot cauldron of cheese? Still not ready to share? We get it. More cheese for you!

2¾ CUPS [660 ML]	UNSWEETENED SOY MILK
2 CUPS [480 ML]	REFINED COCONUT OIL, MELTED
1 TSP	WHITE WINE VINEGAR
1 TBSP	COOKING SHERRY
1 TBSP	TAHINI
½ CUP [65 G]	TAPIOCA FLOUR
2 TBSP	SALT
3 TBSP	NUTRITIONAL YEAST FLAKES
2 TSP	WHITE MISO PASTE
1 TSP	GROUND MUSTARD

HOW TO MAKE IT

In the bowl of a blender, combine the soy milk, coconut oil, vinegar, sherry, tahini, tapioca flour, salt, nutritional yeast, miso, and mustard. Process until smooth, scraping down the sides with a rubber spatula.

Empty the contents of the blender into a medium saucepan and cook over medium heat. To prevent burning, use a rubber spatula to scrape the bottom and sides of the pan constantly as the cheese begins to congeal and thicken. Cook until glossy and the cheese registers 180°F [82°C] on a probe thermometer.

Serve immediately or store in an airtight container for up to 1 week.

WHEN YOU DIP, I DIP, WE DIP!

What do you dip in fondue, you ask? You can do veggies, fruits, vegan meats, and—most important—BREAD!

Here are some of our favorite foods to immerse in this cheesy fondue:

Veggies: Broccoli, asparagus, cauliflower, bell peppers

Fruits: Apples, grapes, pears

Vegan meats: Sausages, steak chunks, chicken

Bread: Focaccia, French bread, raisin bread, garlic bread

Banana Pecan French Toast Bake

MAKES ENOUGH FOR A CROWD (TRUST US)

It's a breakfast. It's a dessert. It's a family favorite. And it takes less than 15 minutes to prep. Prepare the base the night before, and you'll be halfway to breakfast nirvana in the morning. Sip a mimosa or a Bloody Mary and watch hungrily as the candied topping bubbles to perfection.

For the Overnight Base	
1	FRENCH BAGUETTE
5 EGGS' WORTH	FOLLOW YOUR HEART VEGAN EGG
1¾ CUPS [420 ML]	NONDAIRY CREAMER
1 CUP [240 ML]	NONDAIRY MILK
3 TBSP	GRANULATED SUGAR
1 TSP	VANILLA EXTRACT
½ TSP	GROUND CINNAMON
¼ TSP	GROUND NUTMEG
⅛ TSP	KOSHER SALT
For the Topping	
2 CUPS [240 G]	CHOPPED PECANS
2	BANANAS, SLICED
1 CUP [220 G]	VEGAN BUTTER
1 CUP [200 G]	BROWN SUGAR
2 TBSP	MAPLE SYRUP, PLUS MORE FOR SERVING
½ TSP	GROUND CINNAMON
½ TSP	GROUND NUTMEG
2 CUPS [290 G]	CHOPPED VEGAN BREAKFAST SAUSAGE (IF YOU CAN'T GET OURS, WE LIKE BEYOND BREAKFAST SAUSAGE)

HOW TO MAKE IT

Grease a 9 by 13 in [23 by 33 cm] baking dish.

To make the base the night before: Slice the baguette into 1 in [2.5 cm] slices and fill the baking dish, overlapping the slices.

In a large mixing bowl, combine the vegan eggs, nondairy creamer, nondairy milk, granulated sugar, vanilla, cinnamon, nutmeg, and salt; whisk until evenly mixed. Pour the mixture over the bread, covering all pieces thoroughly. You may have to push some areas down. Cover the pan and refrigerate until morning.

The next morning, preheat the oven to 375°F [190°C].

To make the topping: In a large bowl, combine the pecans, bananas, vegan butter, brown sugar, maple syrup, cinnamon, and nutmeg; stir until combined.

Grab that baking dish with the base and sprinkle the breakfast sausage over it, pushing the sausage into nooks and crannies with a spoon.

Pour the topping evenly over the baking dish. Bake for 45 minutes, until fluffy and golden brown. Serve with warm maple syrup. Store leftovers in an airtight container in the refrigerator and enjoy within 3 days.

CHAPTER

6

Snacks

Who loves snacks? *Weeeeee dooooooo!* Nothing kicks off a meal like an appetizing appetizer. And truly, what else gets a party rolling like a wheel of bite-size treats? Starters have to be the most appealing part of basically any restaurant menu, and we've been known to order a few to make our own little personal potluck. From crispy fried snacks to decadent dips to fluffy bread, what's not to love? We know, sometimes it seems like those inventive hors d'oeuvres are as difficult to make as those fancy French words are to spell. But we assure you, you can do it. Start here. Really, you're going to do great! You'll be impressing the noshers in your life in no time.

Smoky Reuben Croquettes

MAKES 10 TO 12 CROQUETTES

Imagine juicy morsels of smoky corned beef wrapped, battered, and fried. Now, imagine those morsels all bound up with kraut for a little taste bud tickle. On second thought, do you even want to share these?

For the Rueben	
12 OZ [340 G]	VEGAN CORNED BEEF, PASTRAMI, OR SALAMI
1½ CUPS [120 G]	SHREDDED VEGAN SMOKED GOUDA
1 CUP [240 G]	VEGAN CREAM CHEESE
¾ CUP [180 G]	SAUERKRAUT
⅓ CUP [80 G]	VEGAN MAYONNAISE
3 TBSP	CHOPPED GREEN ONION
For the Batter and Coating	
2 CUPS [280 G]	ALL-PURPOSE FLOUR
	SALT
	FRESHLY GROUND BLACK PEPPER
1 RECIPE	VEGAN BUTTERMILK (PAGE 207)
2 CUPS [120 G]	PANKO BREAD CRUMBS
	OIL, FOR FRYING (WE USE VEGETABLE OIL)
	HOT HONEE MUSTARD (PAGE 217), FOR SERVING (OPTIONAL)
	THAT YUMMI YUMMI SAUCE THOUGH . . . (PAGE 214), FOR SERVING (OPTIONAL)

HOW TO MAKE IT

To make the Reuben: To a food processor, add the vegan corned beef, vegan Gouda, vegan cream cheese, sauerkraut, vegan mayo, and green onion and pulse until the ingredients are mixed well. Do not puree completely; you want some chunkiness. Remove the processor blade and set aside.

To make the batter and coating: Gather three shallow bowls. In one, add the flour, season with salt and pepper, and stir well. To the second bowl, add the vegan buttermilk and put the panko in the third.

In a heavy-bottom pan, add enough oil to fill the bottom third of the pot. (If using a home deep-fryer, add oil to the fill line.) Heat the oil until it registers 350°F [180°C] on a probe thermometer. If you don't have a deep-fryer or thermometer, test the oil by carefully adding a drop of water; if it sizzles, it's ready.

With a tablespoon, scoop one heaping spoonful into your hand of the Rueben mixture and roll into round balls.

Carefully roll each ball in flour, then coat it in the buttermilk mixture, and finally roll in the panko. Carefully drop into the hot oil.

CONT'D

Fry in batches of three or four croquettes, ensuring that each ball is completely submerged. Fry until golden brown.

Serve with Hot Honee Mustard and/or Yummi Yummi sauce. The more sauces, the merrier!

Store in an airtight container in the refrigerator and enjoy within 5 days.

Pro Tip

When rolling the Reuben balls, make sure that your hands aren't so warm that they melt the cheese. If they are, run them under some cold water between scoops.

Nashville Hot Popcorn Chicken

SERVES 2 TO 4

You know there's just something about fried chicken. No one needs a scientific study to tell you that. Now, shrink it, make it spicy, and BOOM! You have the snack that Southern summertime dreams are made of.

Start with	
1 LB [455 G]	CHICKEN CUTLETS [PAGE 37] OR PRESSED TOFU, CUT INTO 1 IN [2.5 CM] PIECES [SEE PRO TIP]
2 RECIPES	VEGAN BUTTERMILK [PAGE 207]
For the Batter	
2 CUPS [280 G]	ALL-PURPOSE FLOUR
1 TBSP	SALT
1 TBSP	BLACK PEPPER
ONE 12 OZ [360 ML] BOTTLE	JUST EGG PLANT-BASED EGG REPLACER
½ CUP [120 ML]	HOT SAUCE
For the Nashville Hot Butter	
½ CUP [110 G]	VEGAN BUTTER, MELTED
3 TBSP	CAYENNE PEPPER
1½ TBSP	BROWN SUGAR
1½ TSP	PAPRIKA
1 TSP	GARLIC POWDER
	OIL, FOR FRYING
	HOT HONEE MUSTARD [PAGE 217], FOR SERVING [OPTIONAL]
	CREAMY RANCH [PAGE 221], FOR SERVING [OPTIONAL]

HOW TO MAKE IT

Toss the vegan cutlet pieces with the vegan buttermilk. Refrigerate for at least 2 hours, or overnight.

To make the batter: In a shallow bowl, whisk together the flour, salt, and pepper. In another shallow bowl, whisk together the vegan egg and hot sauce.

Remove the chicken pieces from the buttermilk. Dip in the flour mixture, shaking off excess, then dip in the egg mixture, and then in the flour mixture again. Place the coated chicken on a baking sheet. Let sit, uncovered, in the refrigerator for at least 15 minutes.

Meanwhile, to make the hot butter: In a medium bowl, mix together the vegan butter, cayenne, brown sugar, paprika, and garlic powder; set aside.

Place a cooling rack over a baking pan; set aside. If you don't have a cooling rack, line a pan with paper towels.

In a heavy-bottom pan, heat 3 to 4 in [7.5 to 10 cm] of oil until it registers 350°F [180°C] on a probe thermometer. If you don't have a thermometer, test the oil by carefully adding a drop of water; if it sizzles, it's ready.

CONT'D

Fry the chicken in batches until golden brown and its internal temperature reaches 165°F [74°C], 5 to 8 minutes depending on the thickness. Transfer the fried chicken pieces to the prepared rack.

Brush the chicken generously with the hot butter mixture.

Serve with Hot Honee Mustard or Ranch Dressing, if desired.

Store leftovers in an airtight container in the refrigerator and enjoy within 5 days.

Pro Tip

You can sub tofu for the chicken if you'd like. Wrap the tofu block in paper towels and press it under a cutting board or heavy pot or pan until most of the water is drained from it. Wrap up the tofu in plastic wrap or reusable food wrap and freeze overnight. When you're ready to use it, just pull it out and thaw. This process will give it a different texture, making it perfect for a chicken substitute.

Sham & Eggs Musubi

MAKES 5 MUSUBIS

They say that the perfect food doesn't exist, but we'd like to counter that silly assumption with our brand-new invention. This musubi comes packin' with layers of goodness, including a vegan tofu egg patty like you've never had it before, crispy rice cakes, and Sham (our meat-free take on the famous canned ham). Top it with the soon-to-be famous ketchup caviar. You're welcome.

Start with	
5 SLICES	SHAM [PAGE 51]
For the Tofu Egg	
½ BLOCK [225 G]	EXTRA-FIRM TOFU
3 TBSP	OLIVE OIL
1 TBSP	NUTRITIONAL YEAST FLAKES
1¼ TSP	KALA NAMAK [BLACK SALT]
¾ TSP	GRANULATED GARLIC
¾ TSP	GROUND CUMIN
¾ TSP	GROUND TURMERIC
For the Crispy Rice Cakes	
1 CUP [200 G]	UNCOOKED SUSHI RICE
	SALT
	OIL, FOR FRYING
For the Ketchup Caviar	
¾ CUP [180 ML]	WATER
⅓ CUP [85 G]	KETCHUP
¾ TSP	AGAR-AGAR POWDER
1 CUP [240 ML]	VEGETABLE OIL, REFRIGERATED
3 CUPS [720 ML]	COLD WATER
For the Assembly	
2	SUSHI NORI SHEETS
	THAT YUMMI YUMMI SAUCE THOUGH . . . [PAGE 214], FOR SERVING [OPTIONAL]

HOW TO MAKE IT

Preheat the oven to 375°F [190°C]. Grease a baking sheet. Line a plate with paper towels.

Prepare the Sham and set aside.

To make the tofu egg: Drain the tofu and wrap in in several layers of paper towels. Put a cutting board on top of the tofu and a light weight of some kind to remove as much moisture as you can, changing the paper towels if necessary. Press the tofu for up to 1 hour.

In a medium bowl, combine the olive oil, nutritional yeast, kala namak, granulated garlic, cumin, and turmeric. Whisk and set aside.

Slice the tofu into ½ in [1.2 cm] slices and place them on the prepared baking sheet. Coat the tofu with the oil mixture using a pastry brush or a spoon.

Bake, uncovered, for 30 minutes, or until the tofu is firm and slightly browned.

To make the crispy rice cakes: Cook the rice according to the package instructions, adding salt to the water. Set aside.

CONT'D

Shape your rice cakes into five 2 by 3 in [5 by 7.5 cm] rectangles (see Pro Tip).

In heavy-bottom skillet, heat 1 in [2.5 cm] of oil until it registers 350°F [180°C] on a probe thermometer. If you don't have a thermometer, test the oil by carefully adding a drop of water; if it sizzles, it's ready. The oil should be hot enough that the rice cakes will cook quickly and don't soak up too much oil.

Fry each rice cake on all sides until golden and crisp. Use long tongs to turn the rice cakes to avoid splashing the hot oil.

Put the fried rice cakes on the prepared plate to drain extra oil and set aside.

To make the ketchup caviar: In a small saucepan, whisk together the water and ketchup. Add the agar-agar and continue whisking until there are no lumps. Bring to a boil over medium-high heat and then remove from the heat.

Fill a pipette or dropper with the ketchup mixture. Put the cold oil in a medium bowl. Place single droplets, one by one, into the cold oil so they form beads. Continue this process until all the ketchup mixture is used.

Place the cold water in a medium bowl. Using a slotted spoon, carefully remove the ketchup droplets, straining out as much of the oil as you can, and transfer to the cold water. Let rest for a few minutes and then gently stir the water to remove excess oil.

You can store the Ketchup Caviar in the refrigerator for up to 7 days if you don't plan on using it right away.

To assemble: Separate the nori sheets along the perforated lines. If your sheets aren't perforated, use scissors to cut the nori into 3 in [7.5 cm] strips.

On a cutting board, place nori strips side by side. In the center of the nori strip, in the following order, stack one slice of Sham, one slice of tofu egg, and one crispy rice cake. Fold the nori over the stack and seal the strip using a little water on your fingertip. Flip over and voilà! Spoon a small pile of your Ketchup Caviar on top and serve.

Extra Credit

We like to have some of Kale's Yummi Yummi sauce (page 214) on the side for dipping.

Pro Tip

You can find affordable square cookie cutters online, but anything that you can use to make a square or rectangle with the rice will work fine, such as a small food storage container or even a similar shaped cookie cutter.

Minneapolis-Style Cheezy Artichoke Dip

SERVES 4 TO 8

This is such a decadent dip you'll think you've committed a crime. It's a savory delight with enough layers to keep you warm all winter long, but we've been known to serve it in any season and for lots of reasons. It's that kind of dip.

TWO 15 OZ [430 G] CANS	ARTICHOKE HEARTS, DRAINED AND CHOPPED
1½ CUPS [165 G]	SHREDDED VEGAN PARMESAN CHEESE
1 CUP [240 G]	VEGAN MAYONNAISE
ONE 4 OZ [115 G] CAN	RED CHILES, DRAINED
ONE 4 OZ [115 G] CAN	GREEN CHILES, DRAINED
3	GARLIC CLOVES, CHOPPED
1 TBSP	CHOPPED PIMENTOS
1 TSP	NUTRITIONAL YEAST FLAKES
1 TSP	RED PEPPER FLAKES
	GARLIC TOAST, FOR SERVING [SEE PRO TIP]

HOW TO MAKE IT

Preheat the oven to 350°F [180°C].

In a large bowl, combine the artichoke hearts, 1 cup [110 g] of the vegan Parmesan, the vegan mayo, red and green chiles, garlic, pimentos, nutritional yeast, and red pepper flakes. Make sure everything is mixed well. Spoon into an ovenproof ramekin or baking dish.

Top with the remaining ½ cup [55 g] of Parmesan and bake until bubbly, about 30 minutes.

Change your oven setting to high broil and broil for an additional 2 to 3 minutes, until lightly browned, keeping a close eye on it so that it doesn't burn.

Serve immediately with garlic toasts for dipping.

Pro Tip

For the bread, we like to use a baguette, halved lengthwise. Rub the baguette halves with garlic and brush with olive oil. Slice at an angle and place on a baking sheet. Bake at 350°F [180°C] for 10 minutes.

Nana's Chamorro Sweet Bread

MAKES 24 ROLLS

Float away on fluffy, cloudlike puffs of bread. Nana's bread always had the perfect puffiness, which might have something to do with her secret bread-rising ritual: she always put her bowl of dough in a paper grocery bag and put the bag in the bathroom. Bathrooms on Guam are always quite warm, because, well, Guam is really hot and humid, and it all seems to concentrate in this small space. Sure, if you like, you can skip the bathroom part and just put the bowl in a warm place. We kinda like the bathroom step. *Tradition!* Tradition.

ONE ¼ OZ [7 G] PACKET	DRY YEAST
¼ CUP [50 G] PLUS 1 TSP	SUGAR
¼ CUP [60 ML]	WARM WATER
¼ CUP [55 G]	VEGAN BUTTER, PLUS MORE FOR BRUSHING
½ CUP [120 ML]	NONDAIRY MILK
½ CUP [60 ML]	JUST EGG PLANT-BASED EGG REPLACER
2½ CUPS [350 G]	ALL-PURPOSE FLOUR, PLUS MORE IF NEEDED
1 TSP	SALT

HOW TO MAKE IT

In a small bowl, mix together the yeast, 1 tsp of the sugar, and the warm water until the sugar and yeast are dissolved. Let stand for 10 minutes.

Meanwhile, in a small saucepan, melt the vegan butter and nondairy milk, being careful not to let it boil. Let it cool a bit. Add the vegan egg to the milk mixture and stir to combine.

Once the yeast has proofed, or developed a creamy foam, add the milk and egg mixture to it and stir to combine.

In the bowl of a stand mixer fitted with a dough-hook attachment, combine the flour, the remaining ¼ cup [50 g] of the sugar, and the salt. Pour in the liquid mixture. On medium speed, mix the dough just until it begins to lightly pull away from the sides of the bowl. If the dough appears to be sticky, add in more flour 1 Tbsp at a time, until it pulls away from the sides of the bowl. Be very careful to not use too much flour, or your bread will come out tough.

CONT'D

Once you've achieved the proper texture, set a timer and process the bread in the stand mixture on medium speed for 5 minutes.

Meanwhile, grease a medium mixing bowl. When the timer goes off, turn off the mixer and place the bread in the greased bowl. Cover with plastic wrap. Let the bread rest (in the bathroom or not) for 1 hour; it should double in size.

In the meantime, grease a 9 by 13 in [23 by 33 cm] baking dish and listen to a good podcast.

Once the dough has doubled, put it onto a clean and floured countertop and give it a punch. Cut the dough into twenty-four pieces and roll them into balls. Place the balls side by side in the pan (six rolls across and four down). Cover with plastic wrap and let stand for at least 1 hour or until the rolls double in size again.

Meanwhile, preheat your oven to 375°F [190°C].

Once those rolls are good and puffy, remove the plastic wrap, brush the tops with melted vegan butter, and bake on the middle rack for 20 to 25 minutes, until the tops are golden.

Brush with more butter and serve. Store leftovers in an airtight container at room temperature for up to 3 days.

Pro Tip

We like to use this recipe for dinner rolls but also as slider buns. If you're looking to sweeten them up, then cream ¾ cup [165 g] vegan butter with 3 Tbsp sugar and spread the mixture on top of the bread right when you take it out of the oven.

In the first years of the shop's existence, we would often work all night long, tirelessly trying to make enough food to fill the cases for the next day—and it was only then that the kitchen would be quiet enough for Aubry to put on one of our podcast "friends" to tell us stories of terror and wonder that made the overnight shift seem like a blink of an eye. Here's some of our favorite friends that we've met through the years. Share them with your real-life friends when you're cookin' or snackin'!

Darkness Radio and Beyond the Darkness

Whether stirring cheese at 3 a.m. or driving back from an event hours away, it was the voices of *Darkness*, namely Dave Schrader and Tim Dennis, that took us far away from the kitchen to . . . the darkness . . . at the edge of town. Whether it was "ParaShare Monday" or "True Crime Tuesday," this dynamic duo had us on the edge of our seats. But more than anything, it felt like we had a few friends that were right there in the kitchen with us every step of the way.

Hardcore History

Dan Carlin has a way of taking the often-dry subject of history and making it so compelling that you feel like you're watching a Hollywood movie. It also made us understand that no matter how hard things got for us and how much we had to work, it would pale in comparison to the blights and terrors people experienced pretty much all the time before the modern era.

The Last Podcast on the Left

It's hard to inject humor into such subjects as serial killers, death cults, and the occult, but Ben Kissel, Henry Zebrowski, and Marcus Parks have found a way. We never learned so much and laughed so hard at the same time and certainly never thought we'd find new "friends" we like as much as we like *Darkness* Dave and Tim again, but *LPoTL* has been doing it for years—and their content keeps getting better and better.

Panang Bird's Nest

SERVES 4 TO 6

When Kale was a child, the "mystery meat" that filled the "bird's nest" dish on the menu at our local Thai restaurant made up 70 percent of his body weight. After much trial and error, he's gone and made a vegan version that's even tastier than the original. But don't say we didn't warn you about the addictive nature of the nest. Damn it. Make at your own risk.

4	DRIED WOOD EAR MUSHROOMS
4 OZ [115 G]	VEGAN EGG NOODLES OR EQUIVALENT
1 TBSP	MINCED FRESH CILANTRO
1 TBSP	MINCED GARLIC
¾ TSP	FRESHLY GROUND BLACK PEPPER
8 OZ [230 G]	UNCOOKED VEGAN GROUND BEEF [PAGE 33]
1 TSP	SALT
¼ CUP [40 G]	FINELY CHOPPED BAMBOO SHOOTS
¼ CUP [45 G]	FINELY CHOPPED WATER CHESTNUTS
1 TBSP	PANANG CURRY PASTE
1	VEGAN EGG, BEATEN
1 TBSP	CORNSTARCH
3 CUPS [720 ML]	VEGETABLE OIL
	SWEET CHILE SAUCE, FOR SERVING
	SOY SAUCE, FOR SERVING

HOW TO MAKE IT

Soak the mushrooms in water to cover for about 20 minutes. Remove and discard the stems and mince the caps.

Meanwhile, soak the dry noodles in hot water to cover for about 15 minutes. Drain and set aside, tossing them occasionally to prevent sticking.

Using a mortar and pestle or food processor, grind the cilantro, garlic, and pepper into a paste.

In a medium bowl, combine the vegan ground beef with the paste. Add the salt, bamboo shoots, water chestnuts, curry paste, vegan egg, and cornstarch; stir to combine.

In a wok or medium saucepan, heat the oil until it registers 350°F [180°C] on a probe thermometer. If you don't have a thermometer, test the oil by carefully adding a drop of water; if it sizzles, it's ready.

Shape the meat mixture into balls using a tablespoon, then wrap each meatball completely with noodles. Press down on the wrapped ball to ensure it sticks together.

CONT'D

Fry the balls in batches until the noodles are golden brown, about 4 minutes each.

Serve with sweet chile sauce or a bit of soy sauce. Leftovers can be stored in an airtight container in the refrigerator for up to 1 week. Revive them in an air fryer before enjoying!

CURRY SOME FLAVOR

Curry is a Thai staple—and we're pretty sure we wouldn't want to live in a world where it doesn't exist—but while a lot of folks have a shaker of the powder in their cupboard, fewer know about the paste. It has the same spices as curry powder—turmeric, chile powder, and cumin—then goes the extra mile with oil, garlic, lemongrass, ginger, and chiles. You can choose your color: rich and fiery red, mild and fresh green, or slightly sweet and spicy yellow. And then there's the panang curry, which invites peanuts into the mix. The result is a paste with a nutty, mellow flavor and a creamy texture. Now, any curry is a good curry in our book, but we're funny for the complexity of panang.

Tofu Appetizer

SERVES 4

Listen, we're walking on thin ice with this one. We've been getting takeout from the same restaurant (Lucky Dragon Riverside, *babyyyyyy*) just about every week for the last nine years. And every week we get the tofu appetizer. And the *only* reason we're even attempting to re-create it is because many of you don't live in Minneapolis. And if you come to our city and you don't go to Lucky Dragon for their version, so help us we will [censored].

14 OZ [400 G]	FIRM TOFU
1 TSP	SALT
1 TSP	WHITE PEPPER
½ TSP	SUGAR
¼ TSP	CHINESE FIVE-SPICE POWDER
4 TBSP [35 G]	CORNSTARCH
2 TBSP	ALL-PURPOSE FLOUR
¼ CUP [60 ML]	VEGETABLE OIL
5	GARLIC CLOVES, MINCED
1	SHALLOT, FINELY CHOPPED
1 TBSP	FRESH CILANTRO, CHOPPED
	KALE'S BIRTHDAY OIL, LLC [PAGE 227], FOR SERVING [OPTIONAL]

HOW TO MAKE IT

Wrap the tofu in several layers of paper towels. Stack a cutting board and a light weight of some kind on top of the tofu for up to 1 hour to remove as much moisture as you can, changing the paper towels if necessary.

Slice your tofu into ½ in [1.2 cm] slices. Trim the slices into 1½ by 2 in [4 by 5 cm] rectangles and place in a large bowl.

In a small bowl, combine the salt, white pepper, sugar, and five-spice powder. Set aside half of this mixture, then add 2 Tbsp of the cornstarch and the flour; stir to combine. Toss the tofu in the mixture for 1 minute, then add the remaining 2 Tbsp of cornstarch and toss again. This will make the tofu extra crispy.

In a wok over high heat, add the oil. Once heated, add the minced garlic, frying until golden brown—this'll happen in less than a minute, so take care not to let it burn. Transfer the garlic to a paper towel with a slotted spoon and set aside.

In the same oil, add the tofu and fry over high heat until golden brown and crispy, making sure to turn each piece for even cooking. Set the cooked tofu aside.

CONT'D

Drain the oil from the wok, leaving only enough to coat the wok well.

In the wok over medium-high heat, stir-fry the shallots for about 30 seconds until fragrant, then add the crispy tofu, cilantro, and fried garlic. Toss for about 1 minute.

Sprinkle the reserved salt-spice mix over the tofu and toss for another 15 seconds.

Serve hot with Kale's Birthday Oil, LLC, if desired.

CHAPTER
7

Sandwiches

The humble sandwich has come a long way since people first thought to wedge something between two slices of carbohydrates in order to eat it faster. Besides, there's something about that whole portable food package that makes it much greater than the sum of each piece eaten separately. We think Aristotle said that, or maybe it was the Earl of Sandwich. Regardless, in this chapter, you'll find some of our favorite sandwiches. These recipes were inspired by world cuisine, and you'd be hard-pressed to find a vegan version of any of them.

Triple-Dipped Double-Down Fried Chicken Sandwich

MAKES 6 SANDWICHES

It's 120°F in the shade, your deep-fryers are piping hot, strange sounds are blasting at you from every direction, and you have fourteen people in face paint waiting for their Instagram moment with their Double-Down Fried Chicken Sandwiches. Damn right you're a vegan butcher at Coachella. When we made our culinary debut at Coachella, we knew we had to swing for the fences. A few festivals, thirteen grease burns, and thousands of sandwiches later, it's time for you, dear reader and potential culinary hero, to take the torch.

Start with	
1 RECIPE	CHICKEN CUTLETS [PAGE 37]
For the Dry Dredge	
3 CUPS [420 G]	ALL-PURPOSE FLOUR
¼ CUP [30 G]	POWDERED SUGAR
¼ CUP [20 G]	NUTRITIONAL YEAST POWDER
1 TBSP	ONION POWDER
1 TBSP	GRANULATED GARLIC
1 TBSP	PAPRIKA
1 TBSP	SALT
1 TBSP	FRESHLY GROUND BLACK PEPPER
For the Wet Dredge	
3 CUPS [720 ML]	UNSWEETENED PLAIN SOY MILK
1½ CUPS [210 G]	ALL-PURPOSE FLOUR
1 TBSP	BAKING POWDER
1 TBSP	SALT
1 TBSP	APPLE CIDER VINEGAR
For Frying	
4 CUPS [960 ML]	VEGETABLE OIL
For the Sandwich Fixins	
	GARLIC VEGAN MAYONNAISE
	TOMATO SLICES
	RED ONION SLICES
	LETTUCE

HOW TO MAKE IT

Prepare the chicken cutlet recipe and set aside.

To make the dry dredge: In a medium bowl, combine the flour, powdered sugar, nutritional yeast powder, onion powder, granulated garlic, paprika, salt, and pepper.

To make the wet dredge: In a second medium bowl, combine the soy milk, flour, baking powder, salt, and vinegar.

To fry: In a deep pot or fryer over high heat, pour in the oil and heat until it registers 350°F [180°C] on a probe thermometer. If you don't have a thermometer, test the oil by carefully adding a drop of water—if it starts to crackle like crazy, it's ready.

Dredge your chicken by first coating in the dry dredge mixture, then into the wet dredge, making sure there are no dry spots visible. Toss the battered chicken into the dry dredge once more, making sure there are no wet batter spots visible. Three dips are a charm!

CONT'D

Line a plate with paper towels. Now drop the fully battered chicken into the fry oil and stir occasionally until the outside is a lovely golden brown, about 90 seconds. Remember, you'll need two pieces to make the Double-Down, so keep frying until you're out of chicken. Cool the fried pieces on the prepared plate until assembly.

To assemble with fixins: From here, the rest is up to you to assemble your personal best Double-Down. Just remember—the chicken is the bun, the bun is the chicken. If you want to construct yours in true Coachella style, spread some garlic mayo on both "chicken buns"; add in some sliced tomato, red onion, and lettuce; and stick a frilly toothpick in it to hold it together for pictures if you want. Any leftover fried chicken can be stored in an airtight container in the refrigerator, be revived in an air fryer, and enjoyed within a week.

Pro Tip

If you *really* want your Double-Down in true Coachella style, cover yourself in desert dust and make sure you didn't sleep the night before.

The Philly

MAKES 4 SANDWICHES

This Philly cheesesteak is so true to its namesake you might just hear Rocky punching the Liberty Bell in the distance. Many have vied for this title, but we promise you, this is the champion. Just see if it doesn't ring your bell.

Start with	
½ RECIPE	PORTERHOUSE STEAK [PAGE 27]
For the Sandwiches	
4	HOAGIE ROLLS
2 TBSP	SCARBOROUGH GARLIC BUTTER [PAGE 210], AT ROOM TEMPERATURE
4 TBSP [60 ML]	VEGETABLE OIL
1	SWEET ONION, DICED
	SALT
	FRESHLY GROUND BLACK PEPPER
½ CUP [120 ML]	CHEESE SAUCE BASE [PAGE 203], PLUS MORE AS NEEDED
⅓ CUP [20 G]	STORE-BOUGHT FRENCH-FRIED ONIONS
	VEGAN MAYONNAISE, FOR SERVING

HOW TO MAKE IT

Once the steak is prepared, thinly slice it and set it aside.

To make the sandwiches: Split the buns in half lengthwise, spread the garlic butter inside each, then lightly toast on a sauté pan or skillet until golden brown; set aside.

In the same pan over medium-high heat, add 2 Tbsp of the oil. Once heated, add the onion and season with salt and pepper. Cook until caramelized, then transfer the onions to a small bowl.

Add the remaining 2 Tbsp of oil to the pan, increase the heat to high, add the sliced steak, and season with salt and pepper. Once it begins to brown, add the caramelized onions, cheese sauce, and French-fried onions; stir well to combine.

Spread some vegan mayo onto the buns, then divide the steak and cheese mixture evenly among the buns.

If you're feeling fancy, drizzle additional melted cheese sauce on top, but there should be plenty of cheese to go around already. Serve immediately.

Eggs Benedict Burrito

MAKES 1 BURRITO

The mighty eggs benedict is, to me, a perfect brunch food. It has everything I want for brunch on a single plate—salty vegan ham, eggy tofu scramble, crisp spinach leaves, and—crowning it all—a creamy sauce. Now, throw in a tough week survived, a couple of mimosas, and some sunshine, and you're back on the road to happy town. But wait, it gets even better. Wrap up those fancy food items in a tortilla, and you can hold it in one hand, leaving your other hand free to hold that mimosa. —*Aubry*

For the Roasted Tomatoes	
4	TOMATO SLICES
	OLIVE OIL, FOR DRIZZLING
	SALT
	FRESHLY GROUND BLACK PEPPER
For the Tofu Scramble	
1 TBSP	OLIVE OIL
¼ TSP	SOY SAUCE
½ TSP	NUTRITIONAL YEAST FLAKES
¼ TSP	GRANULATED GARLIC
¼ TSP	GROUND TURMERIC
⅛ TSP	WHITE PEPPER
⅛ TSP	KALA NAMAK (BLACK SALT)
½ BLOCK [225 G]	EXTRA-FIRM TOFU, DRAINED AND CRUMBLED
For the Assembly	
1 CUP [240 ML]	BRUNCHY BRUNCH HOLLANDAISE SAUCE (PAGE 225; SEE PRO TIP)
1	FROZEN HASH BROWN PATTY
ONE 12 IN [30.5 CM]	BURRITO-SIZE TORTILLA
5 SLICES [85 G]	VEGAN DELI HAM
2 OZ [55 G]	BABY SPINACH
	SALT
	FRESHLY GROUND BLACK PEPPER

HOW TO MAKE IT

To roast the tomatoes: Preheat the oven to 350°F [180°C]. Arrange the tomato slices on a baking sheet, drizzle with olive oil, and season with salt and pepper. Bake for 5 to 10 minutes or until lightly browned and crisped around the edges.

Meanwhile, to make the tofu scramble: In a small bowl, combine the olive oil, soy sauce, nutritional yeast, granulated garlic, turmeric, white pepper, and kala namak. Whisk until well combined.

In a sauté pan or skillet over medium heat, combine the crumbled tofu and the spiced oil mixture. Stir until the tofu is well coated. Cook until the scramble is golden, 5 to 7 minutes. Set aside.

While it cooks, work on the assembly components: Make the hollandaise recipe. It will come together quickly.

Then, throw that hash brown patty in the oven or air fryer and cook according to the directions on the package. Cut in half.

Lay the tortilla on a cutting board, spread on about 2 Tbsp of the hollandaise sauce, stack the two halves of the hash brown patty, and top with the vegan ham, tofu scramble, roasted tomatoes, spinach, and the remaining hollandaise sauce. Add a dash of salt and pepper and roll on up! For a tidy package, fold in the sides of the burrito as you roll.

Extra Credit

We like to grill the burrito in the skillet just to crisp it up a bit! Serve immediately.

Pro Tip

Make double the amount of hollandaise sauce for dipping.

The Very Best
Mozzarella Stick Sandwich

MAKES 2 SANDWICHES

Visualize a crisp autumn day in Venice. You've stopped to grab a late-afternoon snack and a soothing aperitif. As it turns out, the special of the day is a mozzarella grilled cheese that is battered and fried and served with marinara sauce. What would you do? Would you cry? We're not too proud to admit that we did, in fact, shed a tear when we perfected this sandwich.

10 OZ [280 G]	VEGAN MOZZARELLA CHEESE
4 SLICES	WHITE SANDWICH BREAD
¾ CUP [180 ML]	JUST EGG PLANT-BASED EGG REPLACER
2	GARLIC CLOVES, MINCED
1½ TSP	CHOPPED FRESH FLAT-LEAF PARSLEY
	SALT
	FRESHLY GROUND BLACK PEPPER
2 CUPS [120 G]	PANKO BREAD CRUMBS
	OIL, FOR FRYING (SEE PRO TIP)
	MARINARA SAUCE, FOR DIPPING

Pro Tip

We like to use olive oil for flavor, but any frying oil will do for this gooey-meets-crispy treat.

HOW TO MAKE IT

Cut your vegan mozzarella cheese into slices. Divide the cheese between two slices of the bread, topping with the remaining two slices to make two sandwiches.

In a shallow dish, combine the vegan egg, garlic, parsley, and salt and pepper to taste, and whisk to combine. Put the panko on a plate.

In a cast-iron or heavy-bottom skillet, heat about ¼ in [6 mm] of oil until it registers 350°F [180°C] on a probe thermometer. If you don't have a thermometer, test the oil by carefully adding a drop of water; if it sizzles, it's ready.

Dip each sandwich into the egg mixture first, making sure all sides of the sandwich are coated. Then dredge in the panko until completely coated.

Fry in the oil, turning once, until golden brown and the cheese is melted, 4 to 6 minutes. Serve hot with marinara sauce.

Salt-Roasted Lox

SERVES 6

This recipe is so good we fooled ourselves the first time we tried it. We were thrilled because, let's face it, a bagel with only a schmear of cream cheese seems like a high crime to us now, or at least a bitter disappointment.

4 LARGE	CARROTS, UNPEELED AND WASHED
¼ CUP [60 ML]	OLIVE OIL
1 CUP [220 G]	COARSE SEA SALT
1 TBSP	RICE VINEGAR
1 TSP	FRESHLY SQUEEZED LEMON JUICE
1 TSP	SMOKED PAPRIKA
1 TSP	KELP GRANULES
1 TSP	WHITE MISO PASTE
½ TSP	GRANULATED GARLIC
	VEGAN CREAM CHEESE, FOR SERVING
	CAPERS, FOR SERVING
	FRESH DILL, FOR SERVING [OPTIONAL]
	BAGELS, FOR SERVING

HOW TO MAKE IT

Preheat the oven to 450°F [230°C]. Line a 9 by 13 in [23 by 33 cm] baking dish with parchment paper.

Place the carrots on the prepared pan, drizzle with a bit of the olive oil, and coat with the salt, covering as much of the carrots as possible.

Roast the carrots for 45 minutes, then check to see if they can be easily pierced with a fork. Large carrots will need more time, up to 30 minutes more.

While the carrots are roasting, in a small bowl, mix together the vinegar, lemon juice, paprika, kelp granules, miso, and granulated garlic. Set aside.

After the carrots are done roasting, let cool for a few minutes, then rub off as much salt as you can. Place in an ice bath for 1 minute to stop the cooking process.

Use a paring knife to cut off the salty skin, then use a vegetable peeler to make ribbons of the carrots. Toss the carrot ribbons in the marinade, then let sit for up to 4 hours. Drain.

Serve with vegan cream cheese, capers, and dill on a bagel.

Roti Jane

MAKES 2 BIG SANDWICHES

This recipe is like a lot of Guamanian cuisine—a melting pot of so many beautiful flavors all rolled into one roti. First, you might ask, *What is a roti?* In some cultures, it's a fried flatbread. On Guam, it's a type of thick, coconut-y flour tortilla. You'll find your own delivery system (hoagies are a good place to start)—the important thing is this sandwich's cross-cultural marriage of roti, eggs, veggies, and Sambal Mayo.

2 TBSP	VEGAN BUTTER, PLUS MORE FOR THE SANDWICHES
½ TSP	MINCED GARLIC
1	YELLOW ONION, CHOPPED
½ CUP [70 G]	GRATED CARROTS
2 TBSP	SEEDED AND DICED JALAPEÑO
7 OZ [200 G]	GROUND VEGAN MEAT (WE LIKE HB BACON BRATS OR BEYOND BRATS FOR THIS)
2 CUPS [480 ML]	JUST EGG PLANT-BASED EGG REPLACER
⅛ TSP	KALA NAMAK (BLACK SALT)
4 SLICES	VEGAN CHEESE
2	HOAGIE BUNS
	SAMBAL MAYO [PAGE 218]
	SLICED GREEN ONIONS, FOR GARNISH
	CHOPPED FRESH CILANTRO, FOR GARNISH

HOW TO MAKE IT

In a skillet over medium-low heat, melt the vegan butter. Sauté the garlic, onion, carrots, and jalapeños until the onions are translucent, about 5 minutes.

Add the ground vegan meat and cook until lightly brown, 4 to 5 minutes.

Meanwhile, in a bowl, whisk together the JUST Egg and kala namak. Pour 1 cup of the egg mixture into the skillet and cook over medium-low heat until the egg begins to set. Flip the omelet the best you can to cook thoroughly.

Once the omelet is cooked through to the center, top with 2 slices of the vegan cheese. Cover the pan and cook over low heat for another minute or until the cheese is melted. Set omelet aside and repeat with the remaining egg mixture.

Meanwhile, toast the hoagies. Spread butter and Sambal Mayo on the tops and bottoms.

Put an open bun facedown on each omelet, place an upside-down plate on top, then flip so the sandwich is on the plate.

Top with green onion and cilantro. Close the now overstuffed buns and enjoy!

CHAPTER

8

Bases, Butters,
Sauces, and
Dressings

A good sauce or topping can transform a dish. Heck, the right sauce could turn a plate of plain baked tofu into a symphony. And let's be honest, at the end of an exhausting day when the most you can manage is air-fried chicken nuggets, who's always had your back? Sauces. So, we're topping off this book with some mainstays we've grown to rely on that will grace the shelves of your refrigerator for years—that is, when they're not being used to create or elevate your recipes.

Beef Broth Concentrate

MAKES 6 CUPS [1.4 L]

The backbone of many recipes in this book (and a surprisingly effective, bordering on miraculous, hangover cure), this vegan beef broth concentrate will quickly become a staple in your culinary adventures. Apart from its use flavoring our plant-based meats, it works as a great base for soups and gravies as well.

2 CUPS [480 ML]	SOY SAUCE
½ CUP [120 ML]	APPLE CIDER VINEGAR
½ CUP [120 ML]	SUNFLOWER OIL
2 CUPS [135 G]	NUTRITIONAL YEAST FLAKES
⅓ CUP [55 G]	ONION POWDER
⅓ CUP [50 G]	GARLIC POWDER
¼ CUP [50 G]	GROUND GINGER
2 TBSP	FRESHLY GROUND BLACK PEPPER

HOW TO MAKE IT

In a food processor or blender, combine the soy sauce, vinegar, oil, nutritional yeast, onion powder, garlic powder, ginger, and pepper.

Blend until smooth, making sure to scrape down the sides of the bowl with a rubber spatula for even distribution.

Store the broth concentrate in an airtight container in the refrigerator and use within 3 to 4 weeks for best results. Additional broth concentrate can also be frozen and used within a year.

Chicken Broth Powder

MAKES 3 CUPS [540 G]

If vegan meat is a symphony, then this chicken broth powder is the double bass giving it backbone and structure. The savory nutritional yeast, onion, and garlic powder are rounded out by several herbs and spices—one recipe of this stuff is always good to have in the pantry, both for meatless meats and soups.

½ CUP [90 G]	ONION POWDER
¼ CUP [40 G]	GRANULATED GARLIC
1 TBSP	PAPRIKA
1 TBSP	GROUND SAGE
1 TBSP	DRIED THYME
½ TBSP	DRIED PARSLEY
1 TSP	CELERY SEED
1 TSP	GROUND TURMERIC
5 CUPS [330 G]	NUTRITIONAL YEAST FLAKES
¾ CUP [205 G]	SALT

HOW TO MAKE IT

In a blender or food processor, combine the onion powder, granulated garlic, paprika, sage, thyme, parsley, celery seed, and turmeric. Blend until finely ground.

Add the nutritional yeast and salt. Process until thoroughly combined.

Store the broth powder in an airtight container in the pantry for up to 6 months.

Cheese Sauce Base

MAKE 5 CUPS [1.2 L]

My journey through the world of vegan cheese began with this recipe, and I still make gallons of it every week at the Herbivorous Butcher. I encourage you to experiment with different ratios, binders, and emulsifiers—you never know what sort of magic you can create. —*Kale*

2¾ CUPS [660 ML]	UNSWEETENED SOY MILK
2 CUPS [480 ML]	REFINED COCONUT OIL, MELTED
1 TSP	WHITE WINE VINEGAR
1 TSP	FRESHLY SQUEEZED LEMON JUICE
⅓ CUP [45 G]	TAPIOCA FLOUR
3 TBSP	NUTRITIONAL YEAST FLAKES
2 TBSP	SALT
2 TSP	WHITE MISO PASTE

HOW TO MAKE IT

In the carafe of a blender, combine the soy milk, coconut oil, vinegar, lemon juice, tapioca flour, nutritional yeast, salt, and miso. Process until smooth, scraping down the sides with a rubber spatula.

Empty the contents of the blender into a medium saucepan over medium heat and cook until the sauce is glossy and registers 180°F [82°C] on a probe thermometer. To prevent burning, use a rubber spatula to scrape the bottom and sides of the pan constantly as the cheese begins to congeal and thicken.

Serve immediately or store the sauce in an airtight container in the refrigerator for up to 1 week.

Pro Tip

In some recipes, ingredients can be replaced and changed, but the soy milk and coconut oil in this recipe are vital for its success. Preferably the soy milk you choose will have just two ingredients: soy milk and water. Ingredients like carrageenan and other additives when not used on purpose can adversely affect the end result. At the very least, get one without any added sugar. The coconut oil must be refined—that is, without the flavor and aroma of coconut. If the label reads "virgin," it's usually unrefined, which will leave your cheese sauce tasting a bit more tropical than intended.

Pro Tip

Feel free to play around with the amount of tapioca flour you use. Adding more will simply produce a thicker sauce. And don't let anyone tell you differently—the thickness you prefer your cheese sauce to be is your own damn business!

Kale's Pizza Dough

MAKES ONE 12 IN [30.5 CM] CRUST

I always assumed that making a pizza dough better than most of the restaurants around town was impossible . . . but that was only because I hadn't tried. —*Kale*

2 CUPS [280 G]	BREAD FLOUR, PLUS MORE AS NEEDED [SEE PRO TIP]
½ ENVELOPE OR 1⅛ TSP	INSTANT DRY YEAST
1 TSP	SALT
½ TSP	SUGAR
¾ CUP [180 ML]	WARM WATER
1 TBSP	OLIVE OIL

HOW TO MAKE IT

In a large bowl, combine the flour, yeast, salt, and sugar; whisk thoroughly.

In a small saucepan, heat the water to 100 to 110°F [35 to 43°C]. (This must be precise, so grab your cooking thermometer!) In a large bowl, whisk together the warm water and olive oil. Slowly add to the dry ingredients while stirring.

Transfer the dough to a lightly floured surface and knead until no dry spots remain. If the dough is too sticky, add flour 1 Tbsp at a time. Alternatively, if it's too dry, add water 1 Tbsp at a time. Knead the dough into a smooth ball.

Grease a medium bowl with olive oil, transfer the dough ball to the bowl, and cover with plastic wrap. Place the dough in a warm area and let rise for 1 hour.

Turn out the dough onto a floured surface and let rest for a few minutes before using in a recipe. Use prepared dough within a day or two.

Pro Tip

You can substitute all-purpose flour in this recipe. Just add 1½ Tbsp vital wheat gluten and you're good to go!

Vegan Buttermilk

MAKES 1 CUP [240 ML]

Because buttermilk is in more recipes that you can imagine, here's the easy 1:1 recipe for our vegan version.

1 TBSP	FRESHLY SQUEEZED LEMON JUICE OR APPLE CIDER VINEGAR
1 CUP [240 ML]	UNSWEETENED SOY MILK

HOW TO MAKE IT
In a small bowl, mix together the lemon juice and soy milk. Set aside for 2 minutes to allow it to curdle. Then whisk it again and—voilà!—you have vegan buttermilk.

Better Butter

MAKES 6 CUPS [1.4 L]

This vegan butter bakes into your recipes like a dream, caresses pan-fried goods like a creamy cradle, and *might* be a useful hair product... we're still looking for a willing test participant on that front. Perhaps best of all, it can be tweaked into whatever flavor your heart desires (see page 210 for some of our favorites).

1⅔ CUPS [400 ML]	UNSWEETENED FULL-FAT OAT MILK
1 TBSP	APPLE CIDER VINEGAR
½ CUP [70 G]	SOY LECITHIN GRANULES
1 TBSP	SUGAR
1 TBSP	SALT
1 TBSP	NUTRITIONAL YEAST FLAKES
1 TBSP	XANTHAN GUM
¾ CUP [180 ML]	VEGETABLE OIL
2½ CUPS [600 ML]	REFINED COCONUT OIL, MELTED

HOW TO MAKE IT

In a medium bowl, mix together the oat milk and vinegar.

In a small bowl, mix together the soy lecithin granules, sugar, salt, nutritional yeast, and xanthan gum.

In a blender, combine the oat-milk mixture with the dry ingredient mixture and blend until smooth, scraping down the sides with a rubber spatula to try to blend as many of the granules as possible. Slowly add the vegetable oil; blend until smooth. Next, slowly add the coconut oil and blend for 2 to 3 minutes, until very smooth.

Transfer to an airtight container and refrigerate immediately. Use within 2 to 3 weeks and freeze any extra, using within 6 months.

BETTER BUTTER VARIATIONS

Apple Honey Butter

1 RECIPE	BETTER BUTTER [PAGE 208]
1 CUP [240 ML]	APPLE JUICE
½ CUP [100 G]	SUGAR
½ TSP	FRESHLY SQUEEZED LEMON JUICE

Prepare the Better Butter.

In a small saucepan over medium heat, combine the apple juice, sugar, and lemon juice. Bring to a boil, then immediately lower the heat to a simmer. Cook for 20 minutes until it reaches a honey-like consistency.

Let cool before swirling (do not blend or fully combine) into the Better Butter.

Store in an airtight container in the refrigerator for 2 to 3 weeks or freezer for 6 months.

Scarborough Garlic Butter

1 RECIPE	BETTER BUTTER [PAGE 208]
1 TSP	DRIED PARSLEY
1 TSP	FRESH ROSEMARY
½ TSP	RUBBED SAGE
½ TSP	DRIED THYME
3	GARLIC CLOVES, MINCED

Prepare the Better Butter, then mix in the parsley, rosemary, sage, and thyme. Fold in the garlic until evenly distributed.

Store in an airtight container in the refrigerator for 2 to 3 weeks or in the freezer for 6 months.

Port Wine Medallions

1 RECIPE	BETTER BUTTER [PAGE 208]
½ CUP [120 ML]	PORT WINE
½ CUP [100 G]	SUGAR

Prepare the Better Butter.

In a small saucepan over medium heat, combine the wine and sugar; cook until the sugar is dissolved.

Let cool for a bit, then swirl the mixture into the Better Butter.

Store the port butter in the refrigerator for a few hours until soft and workable.

Use the port butter as is or, to make medallions, tear off a large piece of waxed or parchment paper and lay out 2 cups [480 g] of the port butter onto the paper.

Roll the butter into a log shape as smoothly as possible, trying to avoid wrinkles in the paper.

Store in the refrigerator once more until solid, then remove the paper and slice into medallions. Store any unsliced portion in an airtight container and use within 2 to 3 weeks or freeze and use within 6 months.

Chamorro Barbecue Marinade

MAKES ENOUGH FOR ABOUT 2 LB [910 G] OF VEGAN MEAT

You might find a lot of reasons to whip up this saucy little sauce. We often call on it to marinate our Chicken Cutlets (page 37) or Porterhouse Steak (page 27) before grilling.

2 CUPS [480 ML]	WATER
2 CUPS [480 ML]	SOY SAUCE
1½ CUPS [300 G]	SUGAR
1	YELLOW ONION, CHOPPED
3	GARLIC CLOVES, CHOPPED
2 TSP	MINCED PEELED FRESH GINGER
	FRESHLY GROUND BLACK PEPPER
	RED PEPPER FLAKES

HOW TO MAKE IT

In a large flat dish like a 9 by 13 in [23 by 33 cm] baking dish, whisk together the water, soy sauce, sugar, onion, garlic, and ginger and season with black pepper and red pepper flakes, being sure to dissolve as much of the sugar as possible.

Submerge your desired meat alternative and marinate in the refrigerator for 2 to 3 hours.

Be sure to brush your meat alternative with vegetable oil prior to grilling.

That Yummi Yummi Sauce Though...

MAKES 2½ CUPS [600 ML]

This sauce is so good it was named twice! Yummi Yummi sauce has graced the tables of many a hibachi restaurant all around the world. No one could have known that the sauce was perfection, not just on Japanese food prepared in a flashy fashion, but also on literally everything. And don't be afraid to put it in a squeeze bottle and bring it to Benihana with you ... I know we do.

2 CUPS [480 G]	VEGAN MAYONNAISE
½ CUP [120 ML]	WATER
1 TBSP	SRIRACHA OR HOT SAUCE OF CHOICE
2	GARLIC CLOVES
1 TBSP	KETCHUP
1 TSP	WHITE PEPPER
1 TSP	PAPRIKA
1 TSP	YELLOW MUSTARD
1 TSP	SUGAR
¼ TSP	SALT

HOW TO MAKE IT

In a blender or food processor, combine the vegan mayo, water, sriracha, garlic, ketchup, white pepper, paprika, mustard, sugar, and salt and blend until fully combined, scraping down the sides with a rubber spatula as necessary.

Store in an airtight container and keep refrigerated; use within 2 weeks.

Hot Honee Mustard

MAKES ½ CUP [120 ML]

A little spice complements the winning flavors of this bee-free honey mustard for all kinds of fried chicken, soft pretzels, or—if you're anything like Aubry—lots of other foods!

¼ CUP [60 G]	WHOLE-GRAIN MUSTARD
3 TBSP	HOT SAUCE (OPTIONAL)
2½ TBSP	AGAVE OR MAPLE SYRUP
1 TBSP	YELLOW MUSTARD

HOW TO MAKE IT

In a small bowl, combine all the ingredients thoroughly. Leave out the hot sauce to make equally delicious Sweet Honee Mustard.

Serve with *everything!*

You can make this in batches and store in airtight containers in your refrigerator for up to 2 weeks!

Sambal Mayo

MAKES ½ CUP [120 ML]

This is the perfect mash-up of saucy and sassy. Try the spicy spread on any steak or chicken sandwich to give it a punch or use it as a dip to make raw veggies more exciting. This recipe makes ½ cup [120 ml] of sauce, so you might want to up the amount for double-dippers or to have it on hand for anything else that needs a kick.

½ CUP [120 G]	VEGAN MAYONNAISE
1 TBSP	SAMBAL
⅛ TSP	CAYENNE PEPPER
⅛ TSP	GROUND TURMERIC
⅛ TSP	CHINESE FIVE-SPICE POWDER
⅛ TSP	GARLIC POWDER

HOW TO MAKE IT

In a medium bowl, combine the vegan mayo, sambal, cayenne, turmeric, five-spice powder, and garlic powder.

Use immediately or refrigerate in an airtight container for up to 3 weeks.

Creamy Ranch

MAKES 1⅓ CUPS [360 ML]

This is the perfect dressing and the perfect dipping sauce squeezed into one container of flexible yum. Dip anything *and* everything. Also, feel free to pour it all over your pizza.

1 CUP [240 G]	VEGAN MAYONNAISE
¼ CUP [60 ML]	UNSWEETENED SOY MILK
1 TBSP	APPLE CIDER VINEGAR
2 TSP	GRANULATED GARLIC
2 TSP	ONION POWDER
½ TSP	SALT
½ TSP	FRESHLY GROUND BLACK PEPPER

HOW TO MAKE IT

In a small bowl, combine all the ingredients and whisk well. Store in an airtight container in the refrigerator and enjoy within 1 week.

Warm Bacon Dressing

MAKES 2 CUPS [480 ML]

Our dad doesn't eat a ton of veggies, but he will eat a salad covered in this dressing. That should tell you all you need to know about its deliciousness. Drizzle its greatness on a spinach or wedge salad—or your favorite greens. Bonus points: You can use this recipe as a dip as well.

3 TBSP	OLIVE OIL
5 SLICES	VEGAN BACON, CHOPPED
3	SHALLOTS, CHOPPED
1 CUP [200 G]	SUGAR
¼ CUP [60 ML] PLUS 3 TBSP	WATER
¼ CUP [60 ML]	FRESHLY SQUEEZED LEMON JUICE
1 TBSP	CORNSTARCH
½ TSP	DRIED TARRAGON
¼ TSP	PAPRIKA
¼ TSP	FRESHLY GROUND BLACK PEPPER

HOW TO MAKE IT

Line a plate with paper towels.

In a sauté pan or skillet over medium-low heat, add the olive oil. Once heated, fry the vegan bacon for 4 to 6 minutes, until it just begins to crisp. With a slotted spoon, transfer the bacon from the pan to the prepared plate, leaving behind the bacon grease, and set aside.

In the same pan over medium-low heat, cook the shallots in the bacon grease until soft and caramelized. Stir in the sugar, ¼ cup [60 ml] of water, and the lemon juice. Scrape the skillet to remove any remaining bits of shallots and bacon. Add the crisped bacon.

Make a slurry by mixing together the cornstarch and the remaining 3 Tbsp of water.

Stir the cornstarch slurry into the shallot-bacon mixture and add the tarragon, paprika, and pepper. Cook over medium heat, whisking constantly, until the dressing begins to thicken.

Keep the dressing warm until serving. You can store any leftover dressing in the refrigerator for up to 5 days. Be sure to reheat before use!

Brunchy Brunch Hollandaise Sauce

MAKES 1 CUP [240 ML]

This recipe was created in my kitchen when I was eighteen years old, living on my own, and with about $16 per week to spend on food. I wanted nothing more than a fancy brunch, but my fridge was almost bare, with the exception of Follow Your Heart Vegenaise, Earth Balance butter, and various other condiments and spices. I had to make do. This is the result—and it's still my favorite hollandaise recipe to date. —*Aubry*

1 CUP [240 G]	VEGAN MAYONNAISE
5 TBSP [70 G]	VEGAN BUTTER
1 TSP	FRESHLY SQUEEZED LEMON JUICE
½ TSP	GROUND TURMERIC
½ TSP	YELLOW MUSTARD
¼ TSP	WHITE PEPPER
¼ TSP	CAYENNE PEPPER
⅛ TSP	KALA NAMAK [BLACK SALT]

HOW TO MAKE IT
This recipe can be made on the stove or in the microwave.

To make it on the stove: In a small saucepan over medium-low heat, combine the vegan mayo, vegan butter, lemon juice, turmeric, mustard, white pepper, cayenne, and kala namak; stir well. Cook until heated through, do not boil.

To make it in the microwave: In a small microwave-safe bowl, combine the vegan mayo, vegan butter, lemon juice, turmeric, mustard, white pepper, cayenne, and kala namak; stir well. Cover with a moist paper towel and microwave on high for 30 seconds at a time, stirring the ingredients between each 30-second interval. Do this until heated through. Depending on your microwave, this will take 1½ to 2 minutes. Use immediately.

Kale's Birthday Oil, LLC

MAKES 6 CUPS [1.4 L]

One of the very best and most misunderstood condiments in the world, Kale's Birthday Oil, LLC, was first created as a birthday present for Aubry when my bank account was dry. Made to be paired with the Tofu Appetizer (page 177), it enhances just about everything it is eaten with. Though I once vowed to take the recipe with me to the grave, I put aside this selfish thought and now offer it up as my gift to all of you. —*Kale*

4 CUPS [960 ML]	VEGETABLE OIL
1	YELLOW ONION, FINELY CHOPPED
12	GARLIC CLOVES, MINCED
½ CUP [35 G]	NUTRITIONAL YEAST FLAKES
¼ CUP [45 G]	ONION POWDER
2 TBSP	PREPARED MINCED GINGER
2 TSP	SALT
1 TBSP	PAPRIKA
1	LEMONGRASS STALK, CHOPPED
1 PIECE	GALANGAL, SLICED
8	KAFFIR LIME LEAVES
¾ CUP [85 G]	RED PEPPER FLAKES

HOW TO MAKE IT

In a medium saucepan over medium-high heat, add the oil. Once hot, carefully add the onion and garlic and fry until golden and crisp. Add the nutritional yeast, onion powder, ginger, salt, and paprika to the oil, turn down the heat to low, and stir to combine.

In a spice sachet, place the lemongrass, galangal, and kaffir lime leaves. Tie up tight. Place into the oil.

Add the red pepper flakes to the oil and let it cook over low heat for 30 minutes.

Carefully taste and add a little more salt, if desired.

Let the oil cool, remove and strain the spice sachet, store the oil in an airtight container, and refrigerate. Enjoy within 6 months; it'll get spicier as time goes by.

Enjoy with just about anything. FYI—the sediment at the bottom of the oil is the best part.

Pro Tip

The *LLC* isn't short for "Limited Liability Corporation," but "Luscious, Lucky Chiles." If you're feeling fancy as well, you can leave the spice sachet in with the birthday oil for a few days for an extra turbo boost of Thai flavor.

Butcher-Strength Worcestershire

MAKES 3 CUPS [720 ML]

Equally at home on a steak or in a Bloody Mary, this sauce is an excellent complement to beefy flavors, wherever they're found.

2 CUPS [480 ML]	APPLE CIDER VINEGAR
½ CUP [120 ML]	SOY SAUCE
¼ CUP [50 G]	BROWN SUGAR
2 TBSP	TAMARIND CONCENTRATE
2 TBSP	FRESHLY SQUEEZED ORANGE JUICE
1 TBSP	FRESHLY SQUEEZED LEMON JUICE
1 TBSP	MOLASSES
1 TBSP	ONION POWDER
1 TBSP	GRANULATED GARLIC
1 TSP	DIJON MUSTARD
1 TSP	LIQUID SMOKE
½ TSP	SALT
1 TBSP	CORNSTARCH
2 TBSP	WATER

HOW TO MAKE IT

In a small saucepan over medium-high heat, combine the vinegar, soy sauce, brown sugar, tamarind concentrate, orange juice, lemon juice, molasses, onion powder, granulated garlic, mustard, liquid smoke, and salt; cook, stirring frequently, until the sugar dissolves, about 3 minutes.

Make a slurry by mixing together the cornstarch and water in a small bowl.

Bring the sauce to a boil and add the cornstarch slurry. Lower the heat to a simmer; cook for 5 minutes more.

Store in an airtight container in the refrigerator and use within 6 months.

The Butchers' Fave Vegan Vittles

Times are a-changin'! It's becoming increasingly easy to find vegan versions of basically everything at any grocery store. It's amazing and inspiring—and fourteen-year-old Past Aubry tears up every time a new vegan product is introduced. She always wished but never imagined a world with so many vegan and vegan-leaning humans in it.

We understand that sometimes it's just easier to get the store-bought versions of all these things. These products are handy if you don't have time to make the vegan meats from this book but want to make the ready-to-eat recipes. This list includes our faves. (It's not like they all aren't wonderful, these are just the ones we use most often at home.)

Don't see your favorite on our list? Who cares; you go pick that thing up at the store and use it! You can always order from our website too; we ship to all fifty states and Puerto Rico! (theherbivorousbutcher.com)

Supporting vegan businesses and buying vegan products are small, critical ways you can help further our cruelty-free agenda. And if you have a hometown favorite that you can get at a local shop or farmers' market, you best get out there and support them.

Meats

- **Beef:** Beyond Meat Ground Beef, Viana Cowgirl Veggie Steaks, Blackbird Foods Original Seitan, Upton's Naturals Traditional Seitan
- **Deli Meats:** Unreal Deli Corned Beef, Tofurky Smoked Ham Slices
- **Pork and Bacon:** Beyond Meat Brat, Upton's Naturals Seitan Bacon, BeLeaf Vegan Bacon
- **Poultry:** Tofurky Lightly Seasoned Chick'n, Abbot's Butcher Slow Roasted Chick'n, Alpha Foods Alpha Strips, Tofurky Roast, Butler Foods Soy Curls
- **Sausages:** Tofurky Italian Sausage, Upton Naturals Updogs, Beyond Italian Sausage

Cheeses, Spreads, Eggs

- Miyoko's Butter, salted and unsalted
- Miyoko's Farmhouse Cheddar and Pepper Jack
- Follow Your Heart Sliced Provolone and Mozzarella
- Forager Project Parmesan
- Tofutti Cream Cheese and Sour Cream
- Kite Hill Ricotta and Cream Cheese
- Follow Your Heart Vegan Egg
- JUST Egg Vegan Egg

Aubry & Kale's Pantry Musts

We wouldn't be caught dead without these items in our kitchen. Sometimes we're picky about brand names, in which case we've included those.

- Calrose sushi rice
- Chinese sesame paste
- Edward & Sons beef and chicken bouillon cubes (vegan, of course)
- Japanese golden curry
- JUST Egg (both the liquid type and frozen patties)

- Kelly's Croutons—especially Gourmet Cheezy Garlic Croutons
- Kimlan low-sodium soy sauce
- Lee Kum Kee Chiu Chow chili oil
- LimonCello La Croix (try it!)
- Miyoko's European cultured vegan butter, salted and unsalted
- Refined coconut oil
- Unsweetened soy milk

The Butchers' Tools of the Trade

We're sharing our secrets for putting all kinds of utensils to use, some in the way they were intended to be used, some not.

- **Bain-marie pans:** Is the bain-marie meant to be used as a mold for our deli meats? No, no, it's not. But, sweet heavens, it does work perfectly.

- **Cast-iron skillet:** Just get one already! They're great for frying, doing multiple methods of cooking in one pan, and getting that bit of iron into your diet.

- **Chopsticks, long:** Working with chopsticks makes everything easier because you can pick up one thing at a time and OMG it's the best! We use them when we're frying, making ramen or hot pots, and even mixing vegan eggs!

- **Dim sum pot:** The best at-home vegan meat–steaming device that money can buy, this pot is always consistent. Sure, an Instant Pot can steam, but can it fit two bain-marie pans? We don't think so! (For more on our favorite steaming apparatus, see page 22.)

- **Immersion blender:** Is there anything more fun than transferring boiling-hot food from a pot to a blender? Yes, literally everything is more fun than that. So, let me introduce you to the benefits of an immersion blender. Also known as a stick blender or a hand blender, this little handheld whizzer tucks away in a drawer and blends ingredients in whatever vessel your ingredients find themselves in. So, you can: Make a soup without burning your hands! Whip up a dressing in a bowl without having to scrape around your blender

blades! Fill a kiddie pool with fruit and make a smoothie bath! All right, we'll stop. Do get one of these though.

- **Instant Pot:** To be honest, we were anti–Instant Pot for years, even though some friend or relative would inevitably get one of us one for Christmas every year. After donating the first couple of pots, we finally decided to try one . . . and it was life changing. It makes difficult recipes such as dal as easy as pressing a button. So, although not necessary, it's a pretty great tool for you to have.

- **Meat slicer:** For some recipes like our Deli Bologna (page 46), unless you have the knife skills of a Japanese master sushi chef, you'll need one of these. It has many more uses than just thinly slicing meats though: It can also quickly process onions, tomatoes, you name it. You can find a small countertop model online or at a local kitchen store.

- **Milk frother:** This little gadget is kind of magical! Not only can you use it to froth up milk for an oat-milk latte, but you can also use it to make delicious vinaigrettes and sauces. WIN and WIN!

- **Probe thermometer:** We don't eat meat, but guess what, we still like to eat hot food. Trust us, you want that vegan steak or bowl pizza to be at 160°F when it comes out just for enjoyment's sake.

- **Sifter, mini:** These come in handy for, yes, powdered sugar and cinnamon dusting, but also for straining the herbs out of dressings and sauces.

- **Slotted spoons, large and small:** We all love juice and sauces, but from time to time you might want to plate something, then add the sauce after so you can control that drizzle. Or maybe you just need to snag some olives out of the jar, sans juice. This will be your best friend; it will steal the solids for you so you can make a clean getaway.

- **Spatula, omelet:** We wouldn't have even known that this type of tool existed pre–JUST Egg but we've found you can use it for so much more! Messy, vegan-eggy sandwiches, crêpes, pancakes, all sorts of fun things—and we bet you'll find more uses if you put your mind to it!

- **Spice sachets for boiling:** There are many recipes that call for flavors without wanting the herbs and spices to remain in the dish. A spice bag is basically a reusable tea bag, so you'll be able to use it for multiple things.

- **Spider:** You'll want this wide, shallow skimmer for frying, boiling, and its namesake—saving spiders from drowning in liquid without killing them. You're such a good person!

- **Tongs with silicone tips:** SO IMPORTANT! Don't scratch your good pans and bowls. And also, the shrill sound of metal-on-metal? YIKES!

- **Two-cup glass measuring cup:** You get to measure 2 cups at one time!! And it still has the 1 cup mark!

- **Whisk, large silicone-lined:** Because sometimes we have pans that are non-stick or bowls we don't want to scratch. They work every bit as well as your everyday whisk, and they're wearing a safety suit!

- **Wok:** The wok can replace just about any pot or pan when it comes right down to it, and when stir-frying, there's simply no replacement.

- **Wooden spoons, three sizes:** For us, wooden spoons are life. Stirring a cake mix? WOODEN SPOON! Sautéing veggies? WOODEN SPOON! Lazy and eating vegan mac 'n' cheese out of the pot? WOODEN SPOON!

Acknowledgments

First and foremost, we want to thank Danny Seo for helping us believe in ourselves and holding our hand literally from the beginning of this cookbook process to its finish. We never really fancied ourselves cookbook writers, but we're so happy that we did it.

Danny introduced us to Joy Tutela from David Black Agency who got us through all the nitty-gritty, from the grueling publisher interviews to the contract fine print—all via Zoom! It was a marathon, and we couldn't have done it without her. Having Joy on our team made us feel like we were living in a warm safe hug throughout the entire process.

Through Danny we also met the wonderful Sandy Soria, Rikki Snyder, and Leslie Orlandini. Where to begin with these three heroes!

Sandy, you are a word whisperer, a wonderful Aubry and Kale keeper, and the best cheerleader that we didn't even know we needed. It has been such an incredible pleasure getting to know you and working with you. Please be on our team for life.

Many, many thanks to Rikki and Leslie for turning our recipes into works of art! We've been cooking these meals for so long that we didn't even realize that they could look so incredible in a photograph. Y'all managed (from halfway across the country and during a pandemic) to bring our nearest and dearest recipes to life in full color. For that, we are eternally grateful.

To Sarah and Vanessa at Chronicle Books, thank you for taking a chance on two kooky vegan butchers! We swear we can cook! LOL. We'll make you proud, we promise.

Thank you to Aubry's fearless husband, Dan, for reading through everything without laughing or judging, for being patient during Aubry's fits of hyperactive cooking, for keeping her on task, and, most of all, for tasting version after version of food that you've already eaten dozens of times before.

Thanks to Kale's partner, Erin, for also tasting everything (good or bad), for living through disaster-kitchen time day after day, and for supporting us through this process. Your feedback is nothing if not honest and it made these recipes better than they've ever been before.

Shout-out to our Herbivorous Butcher family for the support—and for trusting us when we brought you strange containers of food and asked you to taste them. ;)

Thanks, Mom and Dad, for birthing us and feeding us delicious food during our youth.

And Nana, though you've been gone for what seems like an eternity, your recipes and legend will live on forever in the food that we cook every single day. We will forever cook meals for people with all the same love that you put into the food you made for us and our family. We love you and miss you.

If you asked us ten years ago if we thought we'd ever write a cookbook, we would have laughed. Hell, if you asked us if we ever thought we'd own a business ten years ago, we would have cracked up. But here we are!

This cookbook is a very honest storytelling of what we have been eating since we were li'l tots. There are no frills here, just good food.

It took a village to get us where we are today, and we're grateful for all the love and support that our family and friends have given us over the years.

Writing acknowledgments isn't easy. We immediately want to thank everyone in the his(her)story of forever who has ever helped us during this roller-coaster vegan butcher adventure. To you all, THANK YOU FROM THE BOTTOM OF OUR HEARTS!

Index